WHERE IN THE WORLD
IS THE CHURCH?

Other Books by the Author

Mission Accomplished
The Agony of Deceit (ed.)
Made in America: The Shaping of Modern American Evangelicalism
Power Religion: The Selling Out of the Evangelical Church? (ed.)
Christ the Lord: The Reformation and Lordship Salvation (ed.)
The Law of Perfect Freedom
Beyond Culture Wars: Is America a Mission Field or a Battlefield?
Putting the Amazing Back into Grace
In the Face of God
We Believe: Recovering the Essentials of the Apostles' Creed
A Confessing Theology for Postmodern Times (ed.)
A Better Way: Rediscovering the Drama of God-Centered Worship
Covenant and Eschatology: The Divine Drama

WHERE IN THE WORLD IS THE CHURCH?

*A Christian View of Culture
and Your Role in It*

MICHAEL S. HORTON

P U B L I S H I N G
P.O. BOX 817 • PHILLIPSBURG • NEW JERSEY 08865-0817

Reissued 2002, with an index, by Presbyterian and Reformed Publishing Company, P.O. Box 817, Phillipsburg, New Jersey 08865-0817.

Printed in the United States of America

Library of Congress Cataloging-in-Publication Data

Horton, Michael Scott.
    Where in the world is the church? : a Christian view of culture and your role in it / Michael S. Horton.
        p. cm.
    Originally published: Chicago : Moody Press, c1995. With new index.
    Includes bibliographical references and index.
    ISBN 0-87552-565-2 (pbk.)
    1. Christianity and culture. 2. Church and the world. 3. Christian life—Reformed authors. I. Title.

BR115.C8 H68 2002
261—dc21

                                          2002025763

To Gary Horton, with gratitude
for a lifetime of friendship and support

CONTENTS

Let me say at the outset that this book is not a sophisticated analysis of either the theological basis of a Christian worldview or the nature of art, science, philosophy, and so on. It is intended for a general audience, and especially for those Christians who struggle with a subculture that stifles rather than encourages their divinely given impulses and ambitions. In that sense, it is pastoral. It is offered with the hope that theologians will learn more about other disciplines and that Christians in those other disciplines will anchor themselves more firmly in biblical theology before they attempt to "integrate" their faith and life. But regardless of where the reader stands in relation to these topics—whether a well-read aesthete or a Christian mother who wants to know if her daughter is safe at Harvard—there will be a few challenges to the prevailing notions in the evangelical world and something here and there to think about.

INTRODUCTION

Sometimes hymns confuse me. I remember being confused as a boy by two popular hymns that seemed to be quite contradictory. The first was, "This World Is Not My Home, I'm Just Passing Through," and the other was, "This Is My Father's World." *If this is my Father's world,* I wondered, *why am I just passing through?*

But hymns were not the only confusing thing in this business about relating to the larger world as a Christian. Christians were expected to justify everything in their lives by its spiritual or evangelistic usefulness. At best, "secular" education, activities, vocations, or pursuits were a necessary evil—in order to make a living, to be able to tithe and give to the missionaries. At worst, they were a distraction from the Christian life. They acted as the Siren's song drawing unsuspecting worldlings to the shoals of unbelief and backsliding. So, those who wanted to be businesspeople looked for employment to Christian organizations or agencies. If we discovered a little Rembrandt in a young artist at church, we put him in charge of the bulletin and (if he was really

good) allowed him to paint the baptistry. Our scientists were expected to advance the cause of creationism—even if cosmology
or the biological and anthropological sciences were not their spe-
cialties. Musicians were expected to join (or form) a praise band
or tour the country's churches—the size of the church, of course,
depending on the degree of one's talent. Over the years, we have
created our own "ghetto" of artists, superstars, and entertainers,
with Christian versions of everything in the world.

These experiences, however, are not unique to this time and
place. The Renaissance and especially the sixteenth-century Reformation were reactions to the medieval way of looking at life.
For the medieval church, philosophy, art, music, and science
had been so confused with religion that one could hardly tell
them apart. Philosophy was not really philosophy: The Renaissance pointed out how different was the medieval church's interpretation of Aristotle and Plato (their favorites) from the actual
writings of the philosophers. If one wanted to be an artist, it was
again to the church that one came for employment, as art was a
tool of preaching or teaching the life and times of Jesus and His
apostles. And the trials of Copernicus and Galileo remind us of
the dangers of saying more than the Bible does about particular
scientific theories.

*The pressure to justify art, science, and
entertainment in terms of their spiritual value or
evangelistic usefulness ends up damaging both the
gift of creation and the gift of the Gospel.*

The Reformation freed Christian men and women to pursue
their divinely appointed callings in the world with dignity and
respect, without having to justify the usefulness of those callings
to the church or its missionary enterprise. Vocation was a gift of
creation. Even non-Christians possessed this divine calling, as
God's image-bearers. Believer and unbeliever alike were intended
to pursue their work with excellence—the one acknowledging

God as the author and goal of such excellence, and the other serving God with one's talents in spite of his or her refusal to acknowledge God as the giver and goal of it all. Against the monastic worldview, the Reformation championed a world-embracing theology that was a major factor in the rise of science, the "Golden Age" of Dutch art and English and Scottish literature, the liberation of politics from the church, the spread of universal literacy and public education, and the cry for civil liberties against the backdrop of widespread tyranny.

Of course, no movement is perfect—there are too many people like us involved! The Reformation is no exception, with its share of mistakes and the foibles of sinful men and women. Nevertheless, the biblical themes that it recovered brought back to God's people a sense of belonging in this world for the time God has given us—but belonging *in,* not *to,* this world.

The pressure to justify art, science, and entertainment in terms of their spiritual value or evangelistic usefulness ends up damaging both the gift of creation and the gift of the Gospel, devaluing the former and distorting the latter in the process. For instance, "Christian music" is often an excuse for inferior artists to make it in a Christian subculture that mimics the glitz and glamour of secular entertainment, including its own awards ceremonies and superstar ambience. That, of course, may not be the intention on the part of a great many artists who set out to contribute to contemporary Christian music, but the industry nevertheless ends up churning out mostly uncreative, repetitive, shallow imitations of popular music. To produce music that conforms to the numbed tastes of a consumer culture is bad enough; to *imitate* commercialized art is wasting one's talents unless one is writing jingles for radio or television. It trivializes both art and religion. That is not to condemn all Christian artists, for there are a number who are both musically and lyrically sophisticated enough to integrate a serious grasp of the biblical message with a creative musical style. Nor is it to become snobs who confuse their own personal tastes with the revealed Word of God. After all, it is often the case that "the truth is written on subway walls," the architectural equivalent of popular music. That is one reason I enjoy popular music from time to time, partly because it is entertaining and evokes memories of days gone by. But it is an inferior, commercially driven (i.e., financially driven) form that rebels against higher standards of artistic expression.

These pressures, however, to create distinctively "Christian" versions of everything in the world (i.e., in creation) assumes that there is something essentially wrong with creation —and that is a theological presupposition that has a far greater hand in shaping evangelical attitudes in all of these spheres than is commonly admitted. We shall explore that underlying position in the following chapters.

Let me say at the outset that this book is not a sophisticated analysis of either the theological basis of a Christian worldview or the nature of art, science, philosophy, and so on. It is intended for a general audience, and especially for those Christians who struggle with a subculture that stifles rather than encourages their divinely given impulses and ambitions. In that sense, it is pastoral. It is offered with the hope that theologians will learn more about other disciplines and that Christians in those other disciplines will anchor themselves more firmly in biblical theology before they attempt to "integrate" their faith and life. But regardless of where the reader stands in relation to these topics— whether a well-read aesthete or a Christian mother who wants to know if her daughter is safe at Harvard—there will be a few challenges to the prevailing notions in the evangelical world and something here and there to think about.

As we begin, I should define a couple of terms. First, we will be using the term "culture" in its widest possible sense, referring both to popular culture (sports, politics, public education, popular music and entertainment, etc.) and high culture (horticulture, academics, classical music, opera, literature, science, etc.). A useful, all-encompassing definition of "culture" in our discussion might be human activity that is intended for the use, pleasure, or enrichment of society. Second, by "the church" I mean the institutional church—"where the Word is rightly preached and the sacraments are rightly administered," as the Reformation declarations put it. When, for instance, it is said that the church must not confuse its mission with the spheres of politics, art, science, etc., it is not at all suggested that individual Christians should abandon these fields (quite the contrary), but is rather to say that the church *as an institution* must observe its divinely ordained mission. This institutional church is meant to be understood as the visible expression of Christ's universal body throughout all ages and in all places. The institutional church has been given the unique commission to preach the Word and make disciples. My use of the term "church," therefore, is not merely a reference to the collective body of individual Christians, but to the living organism founded by Christ and entrusted with His own personal ministry.

Chapter One

■

HOW TO
BE A
WORLDLY
CHRISTIAN

■

I just want to serve the Lord."

What is your first impression of that statement? When a new Christian who has been practicing law for twenty years says that she has decided to "turn her back on the world" and "give her life to Jesus," don't we automatically assume that this entails some sort of radical commitment to a new occupation? Perhaps she will join a Christian legal service or even eschew law altogether for a church-related profession.

We normally regard the passion to serve the Lord as a passion for missions, evangelism, and involvement in the activities and ministries of the institutional church. But it is that assumption that I want us to rethink through these chapters. I want us to consider the possibility that serving the Lord means a renewed commitment to performing one's calling with greater excellence rather than abandoning that calling for a new one.

Some Christians have difficulty understanding their relationship to the world because they perceive that earth is a realm ruled by Satan; therefore, it seems best to concentrate on evangelism and one's own spiritual growth rather than to get caught up in secular activity. Throughout this book we will explore the world-affirming character of evangelical spirituality, from the Reformation to the Puritans and in some contemporary expressions. Especially in the next chapter, we will also attempt to see the importance of keeping our involvement in the world in proper balance.

IS SATAN IN CHARGE?

"The god of this age has blinded the minds of unbelievers, so that they cannot see the light of the gospel of the glory of Christ, who is the image of God" (2 Corinthians 4:4).

From this passage, many over the centuries have concluded that this world is under the control of Satan and his minions. The enormously popular books of many contemporary "spiritual warfare" writers and leaders have contributed to a cosmic dualism between God and Satan, light and darkness, the good and the evil. This has been a recurring aspect of the Gnostic impulse, viewing this world as a cosmic battleground between spiritual forces whose fate must be decided by the skill of worldlings with spiritual know-how. Thus, "spiritual mapping," advocated by a growing number of missiologists, attempts to identify spiritual "hot-spots" of demonic activity with the goal of "binding" the regions' evil oppressors. Of course, it sounds like something out of a medieval book of superstitions, but it is taken very seriously by a good number of evangelical leaders.

The Reformers were alarmed at the revival of the ancient heresy of Manichaeanism in their day, a form of Gnosticism emphasizing this dualism between the "good god" and "bad god." As Calvin points out with regard to this passage, "Paul says elsewhere that 'many are called gods' (1 Cor. 8:5) and David declares that 'the gods of the nations are demons' (Ps. 96:5). . . . As for the Manichaeans this title lends no more countenance to their views than when the devil is called the prince of this world. . . . For the devil is called the god of this world in exactly the same way as Baal is called the god of those that worship him or the dog is called the god of Egypt." These are not really gods, but

are considered such and treated as such by our darkened imaginations. As Luther declared, "The devil is God's devil," so too
Calvin argued that all satanic and demonic influences of evil are
under the sovereign command of God and are held in check by
the true Ruler of the Universe.

C. Peter Wagner relates a case in which a Pentecostal missionary was distributing tracts. The border of Uruguay and Brazil
went through the main street of this small town. When the missionary realized that those on the Uruguayan side would not accept the tracts, while Brazilians would, God gave him "a word":
The "strong man" had been bound on the one side, but not the
other. Wagner offers a further example:

> Omar Cabrera of Santa Fe, Argentina, is one evangelist who
> has taken seriously the need to bind the strong man or to break
> the power of territorial hierarchy. When he goes into a new area
> he shuts himself up alone in a hotel room over a period of four or
> five days for intense fasting and prayer. He does battle with the
> forces of the enemy until he identifies the strong men who have
> ruled over that territory. Then he wrestles with them and binds
> them in the name of the Lord. When this happens he just walks
> into his meeting and announces to the audience that they are free.
> Sick people begin to get healed and lost people begin to get saved
> even before he preaches and prays for them. This kind of power
> evangelism has caused his movement, Vision of the Future, to
> grow from 10,000 to 135,000 believers in five years.[1]

Of course, Scripture records no instances of people getting
saved before hearing the Word preached. Even many popular
evangelical book titles display this fascination with cosmic warfare that bears no affinity to the spiritual warfare described in
Scripture. In Scripture, spiritual warfare takes place on earth, as
Satan attempts to confuse or undermine the believer's confidence in Christ and His imputed righteousness as sufficient for
salvation. In other words, it is a battle for hearts and minds, and
it has to do with truth versus error, belief versus unbelief, faith in
Christ versus faith in something or someone else. It does not focus on "power encounters" and exorcisms, but on the "strong
man" being driven out by a "stronger man" who takes his place.

This popular fad actually bears closer affinity to the "Star Wars" films and is influenced more by the sensationalism of popular culture, with its attraction to the paranormal, than by clear passages.

"Power encounters" is not exactly what Paul had in mind when he referred to Satan as "the god of this world." He was not arguing that a good God rules the spiritual realm, while a bad god rules "secular" and "worldly" arenas. Satan is only the god of this world in the sense that he is served as if he were God. As a minister of wrath, Satan has blinded the hearts of Jews and Gentiles, but it is always with divine permission, and that permission may be withdrawn at any time God wishes.

There is, therefore, no reason to view this world as an inherently evil place, the battleground for control of the planet and of the universe, whose outcome is determined by the demon-binding and "spiritual mapping" of spiritual alchemists. Although we sinful men and women make this world a place of rebellion, evil, and disorder, Satan not only does not have the slightest chance of ultimate victory; he does not, at any time, have victory over God's purposes, nor can he or any other creature frustrate God's plans (Daniel 4:34–37). Nevertheless, he works tirelessly to weaken the believer's confidence in God's grace. The answer to this is a firmer grasp on the Gospel.

The sovereignty of God comforts us in crisis and curbs our pride in triumph.

The sovereignty of God is not only an essential tenet of the Christian faith in particular (and theism in general), but it is also immensely practical for our confidence that God fights our battles for us; evil can never have the last word. At the Cross, we are told, our debt was not only canceled, but "having disarmed the powers and authorities, he made a public spectacle of them, triumphing over them by the cross" (Colossians 2:15). Is it not the height of arrogance, bordering on blasphemy, to suggest that it is the believer's victory over demonic forces rather than Christ's once-and-for-all triumph that secures liberation from bondage? It is by proclaiming the Gospel, Paul declares in his famous passage on spiritual warfare (Ephesians 6), not by taking it upon ourselves to eradicate spiritual darkness, that God's kingdom is extended and Satan's diminished.

Often, our political causes, like our evangelistic crusades, tend to ignore this fundamental truth, so that we sometimes sound as if this latest, greatest movement (the Christian Right in politics or Promise Keepers, the Signs and Wonders movement, or Vision 2000 in evangelism and missions) of our own frenetic activity and ambitious, entrepreneurial projects will achieve the work credited in Scripture to the Cross of Christ. Or, on the other end, if the wrong person occupies the White House, we give the impression that the universe is out of control, as if God depended on us and our machinery for the realization of His kingdom. Very often, the most well-meaning believers engage in these ambitious causes with the best of motives, but the temptation is great to forget, when we lose, that Christ is still King, and, when we win, that we are not.

Of course, this is not to say that Christ's triumph at the Cross eliminates our responsibility to evangelize the nations or to teach them righteousness, but it is to say that the only way we bring this victory to the nations is by proclaiming what Christ has already accomplished, not by our feats of grandeur and glory. For, unlike the "super-apostles," as Paul referred to the Gnostics, "We do not preach ourselves, but Jesus Christ as Lord, and ourselves as your servants for Jesus' sake" (2 Corinthians 4:5).

The sovereignty of God comforts us in crisis and curbs our pride in triumph, reminding us that it is not we who determine the outcome of spiritual battles, but Christ the King who fights for us and has already secured the final victory.

A FEW GOOD EXAMPLES

Given that this is still God's world and He rules in providence even where He does not rule as Savior, how can we become "worldly Christians" in the best sense of that phrase? Perhaps it would help at this point to observe the heritage that we have in evangelical Christianity, not because there were no great examples of faithfulness to this worldly mission before the Reformation, but because that movement restored the world-embracing and world-affirming piety that we find clearly expounded in Holy Scripture.

Martin Luther knew that understanding that the acceptance of the sinner before a holy God was the result of an "alien righteousness" would necessarily lead to revolutions in human relations. Released from the inward focus, the believer was free to embrace the world as a spiritual and godly activity, instead of separating from it with the misunderstanding that he was thereby separating from sinfulness. "For even in the monk's cell," Luther recalled, "I still had that rascal [his own sinful self] right in there with me."

When common laypeople discovered this Gospel, they were so revolutionized by it that they wanted to do everything they could to promote it. Far from leading to moral laxity, it inspired zeal where there had been apathy. In fact, a cobbler asked Luther what he should now do since he had embraced the Gospel. What should his calling now be? Just as for the hypothetical lawyer I mentioned at the beginning who wanted to serve the Lord, this was an obvious question for a medieval person who had been trained to think that a great spiritual experience required special devotion in terms of a sacred calling. The Reformer's response was as surprising to the cobbler as it might be to some of us today: "Make a good shoe and sell it at a fair price." When asked what he would do if he knew Christ were coming back tomorrow, Luther replied, "I would plant a tree." In other words, God is so pleased with our ordinary, faithful activity in this world that Luther no longer felt that he had to be found in prayer or in "spiritual" exercises when Christ returned in order to receive His blessing.

In the Family

Luther is also considered by many historians to have been the father of the view of the family that has become so much a part of a now-vanishing Western heritage. Before, false spiritual-

20

ity had undermined the godly home in the sense that raising a family was not considered an act of service to God in and of itself. It was secular, mundane, common, and, therefore, the most devout Christians would separate themselves from such worldly concerns and concentrate on their own personal spiritual ascent up the ladder of Christian experience and piety. Sexual intercourse was considered a necessary evil for procreative purposes, but Luther and the other Reformers caused no small scandal when they declared that it was meant also for pleasure and communion in the marital relationship. The vignettes of Luther's home life are filled with portraits of a family sitting around the table praying, reading Scripture, and also singing, playing instruments, and playing games.

In Art

In art, things were beginning to change as well, as we will see more fully in our discussion of Christianity and the arts. One can see the transformation by touring a modern museum with a medieval collection and a Dutch Baroque collection. Some years ago, I tried this out on a Roman Catholic friend with whom I was studying human rights in France. We had been reading Paul's epistle to the Romans together, and he was eager to learn more about the Gospel, so one day, when we were touring The Louvre in Paris, we visited the medieval wing and then the Dutch Baroque. Without much direction, he was able to see for himself the different worldviews at work. In the medieval paintings, for instance, the subject was almost always religious. Even when secular subjects (such as pagan myths) were portrayed, biblical characters or images were integrated as if somehow the secular subject required some justification.

The popular paintings of the Madonna and Child, reflecting Byzantine influences, were often iconographic: that is, flat, one-dimensional, and highly ornamented. The obvious intention was to inspire devotion and to teach a moral or spiritual lesson. Not unlike our own day, the image rather than the word was often the means of communication and instruction, so art served a didactic and moral purpose. The church had commissioned the great

21

majority of artistic works, and this is how a talented person would make a living in the medieval world.

Then we moved to the Dutch Baroque section and immediately detected an entirely different outlook on life and religion. First, the majority of the works were secular; that is, they did not intend to preach or teach. They did not try to inform or inspire an otherworldly piety. One is overwhelmed with pastoral scenes, vignettes of common village life, working men and women, families (like Luther's) gathered around the table enjoying each other's entertainments on musical instruments (sometimes with the pastor participating, indicating the church's affirmation of this home life). There are the still life paintings, with bowls of fruit meticulously represented, and there are also haunting scenes, with the poverty of the homeless contrasted with the gaiety of courtly life. This world was an acceptable subject of wonder and study, even apart from somehow teaching a spiritual or moral lesson or converting the lost. And yet, though it was not their explicit purpose, these paintings were illustrations of the differences between Roman Catholic piety in which my friend had been raised (and had rejected) and the evangelical perspective. It gave me an example to explain the Gospel itself and to discuss the ways in which the two different gospels create two distinct worldviews.

Even in the religious paintings, one notices a revolution in worldviews at work. For instance, in the medieval paintings of the Holy Family, there is a flat, one-dimensional portrait. Mary, Joseph, and Jesus are wearing expensive robes and golden halos. After all, the purpose is to inspire devotion, to teach, and to bring the laity into contact with the unseen God. In Rembrandt's portrait of the same subject, he has the Holy Family seated in the corner of a room. The foreground depicts a typical peasant's home and takes up the largest portion of the canvas. By every indication in terms of dress and environment, this is a normal peasant family. The source of light is natural: Instead of emanating from halos, it breaks through a window as natural light from the afternoon sun.

Thus, two important principles are at work: First, there is the acceptance of this world as it really is, created by God, cared for by God, but broken and corrupt. It is utterly realistic and unsentimental. There is real perspective, giving the impression that this is a real family living in a real place, in a real time, and not a spiritualized, ephemeral family with little connection to earthly reality. Part of the perspective is due to the influence of the Renaissance, which rebelled against the medieval worldview and its static view of life and history, insisting instead that the study of history and secular disciplines could be an end in itself, apart from the all-controlling spirituality of the church. But the Reformation exploited this interest in recovering a sense of real history and perspective—not only in recovering the ancient faith, but in describing the real world in real terms again. True, Jesus is God, but the medieval church had so stressed His distance and divinity that the devout had to look to saints and Mary for understanding. The Reformation emphasized the truth that God had become human, bringing dignity to earthly, secular life. In Christ, God had become someone's next-door neighbor. The second principle at work is this: One need not "sanctify" art by demanding that it serve the religious or moral interests of the church. Creation is a legitimate sphere in its own right. The late Dutch art historian Hans Rookmaker, a friend of Francis Schaeffer, summarized it well in the title of his little book, *Art Needs No Justification.*

Although the medieval worldview produced a host of astounding artistic works, beautiful and alluring in their skillful depictions of the religious ideal, the Reformation worldview freed art from its constraints and allowed it to be a purely secular enterprise, to the glory of God. Names such as Rembrandt, Vermeer, de Hootch, Cranach, Holbein, and Dürer loom largely in the history of art, and they gave artistic expression to this outlook. In fact, Albrecht Dürer (1471–1528) was converted to the Gospel and became a student and personal friend of Luther, as the Reformer's preaching had led him "out of great anxieties." Dürer, who had already embraced the Renaissance style over the medieval, felt free now to depict secular subjects in illustrations for new scientific texts, the charts of explorers, and portraits. His woodcuts (such as his famous "Four Horsemen of the Apocalypse") were often religious, but again, in a realistic style. When these artists appealed to biblical stories, the characters were dressed in contemporary clothes and represented actual lives of people from every walk of life, rich and poor. Lucas Cranach, who died in 1553, provided many portraits and altarpieces for evangelical churches.

The Zurich Reformer, Ulrich Zwingli (1484–1531), prohibited art and music in the church because he insisted that the Word and sacraments alone be central. Nevertheless, he himself played instruments and founded the Zurich orchestra. Again and again we see the Reformers' attitude as being far from anti-art or anti-music, but of wanting to liberate the Word in worship and the arts in creation. Luther argued that art and music could be useful in worship, so long as they were not allowed primacy over the Word. "Music is an outstanding gift of God," he announced, "and next to theology. I would not give up my slight knowledge of music for any consideration. And youth should be taught this art; for it makes fine, skillful people."[2] Even schoolmasters must know how to sing, Luther insisted.

While many of the Anabaptists were advocating the overthrow of the arts as "worldly," Luther countered, "I am not at all of the opinion that the arts are to be overthrown and cast aside by the Gospel, as some superspiritual people protest; but I would gladly see all the arts, especially music, in the service of him who has given and created them."[3] A hymn-writer himself, Luther inspired a whole tradition in evangelical hymnody.

In Music

Johann Sebastian Bach's name comes to mind as someone who carried this vision forward. Both his sacred and his secular pieces carried the same signature: "S.D.G."—the Reformation slogan "Soli Deo Gloria" (To God Alone Be Glory), and he had these initials carved into the organ at Leipzig. G. F. Handel declared, "What a wonderful thing it is to be sure of one's faith! How wonderful to be a member of the evangelical church, which preaches the free grace of God through Christ as the hope of sinners! If we were to rely on our works—my God, what would become of us?"[4] In the nineteenth century, a young Jewish musician was converted to Christ and composed his celebrated "Reformation Symphony" in tribute to God's gracious gift. That young man's name was Felix Mendelssohn.

These great artists were able to move freely between the secular and sacred without confusing either, for they were comfortable with reality, whether it was the reality about Creation and the Fall, historical epics, delicate impressions of a foreign land, or the reality of salvation from sin and redemption in Christ. They moved comfortably between the secular and the sacred as legitimate and divinely ordained realms, but they did not confuse them.

The Reformed tradition that was most shaped by the influence of John Calvin also produced a rich artistic tradition. Not only was the Dutch Baroque a tribute to his influence, but the tradition of psalm-singing, largely forgotten in our day, was popularized during his ministry in Geneva. Schoolchildren in France could be heard singing the Psalms on the playground (until the schoolmaster compelled them to stop), and these masterful hymns were sung as far away as Hungary, Poland, Scotland, and Italy during the Reformation. Although Calvin warned against bringing the church back under the ceremonial laws of Israel, which were merely a shadow of the future kingdom and passed away with Christ's advent, he nevertheless encouraged the development of musical societies in the community. For the sacred psalm-singing in the churches, he employed perhaps the most famous poet of the French Renaissance, Clement Marot (1497–1544), to write the text and compose the music with the assistance of Louis Bourgeois.

Even in the dramatic arts, there was a noticeable impact. Most dramatic performances were in the form of medieval morality plays, which often had the same ending: the good being received into glory and those who failed to learn the lesson cast into hell. But the Reformers freed this sphere, too, from its church-related domain. In fact, Calvin's pastoral associate and successor in Geneva, Theodore Beza (1519–1605), wrote the first French tragedy, in between writing his massive theological tomes. The Puritans in England were far from condemning the theater, as an important work by Martin Butler, *Theatre and Crisis, 1632–*

1642 (Cambridge Univ. Press, 1984) has demonstrated. Many were themselves architects of the Shakespearean stage.

In Literature

In the literary arts, the Reformation inspired freedom from churchly constraints as well. In its wake we see the rise of the modern novel, historical studies, and a variety of literary explorations. Luther wrote on a variety of secular subjects, and Calvin even tried his hand at poetry. Calvin's first published work was a commentary, *De Clementia* (Concerning Clemency), a study of the ancient Roman jurist Seneca. Beza wrote political texts that many historians now regard as having had a major hand in shaping modern democratic theory.

A great many disturbing and upsetting changes could take place in our understanding of the universe without overthrowing the infallible revelation of Scripture.

The "Golden Age" of English literature is linked to the Reformation, with names such as Spenser, Donne, Herbert, Milton, and a host of additional luminaries illustrating the enormous influence of that evangelical movement.

In Science

In science, the same spirit prevailed. No better example could be given of the confusion and dominance of the church over the scientific enterprise than the Copernicus affair. While we will leave the discussion of that crisis to the proper chapter, suffice it to say here that when the church confuses Scripture with a particular philosophical system, it can easily speak where Scripture has not spoken and weaken biblical authority when the church's dogmatic assertions are found to be impossible to reconcile with the facts. The church had confused biblical orthodoxy with Aristotle, and when science proved the geocentric cosmology false, many concluded that the Bible had simply been overthrown by the facts.

For the Reformers, the Bible was about Christ, not about the relation of planets. Calvin praised astronomy and cautioned against expecting Moses to give scientific information about the movement of planets and stars. We ought not to "censure Moses for not speaking with greater exactness. . . . Moses wrote in a popular style things which, without instruction, all ordinary persons, endued with common sense, are able to understand; but astronomers investigate with great labour whatever the sagacity of the human mind can comprehend."[5] As the Bible was not to be seen as a handbook for artistic, literary, musical, or political theory, so it was not to be seen as a textbook for science. Everything in Scripture is true, in the sense in which it was intended by its original author, but the purpose of Scripture is not to tell us everything about everything, but to explain—in the most common and basic language possible—the progress of God's saving work in Christ through redemptive history.

This liberated the scientist to pursue his calling without having those who were untrained in the sciences constantly judging his observations. The great Protestant scientists, therefore, believed that the "second book of God," as they referred to creation, would harmonize perfectly with the "first book" (Scripture), since God was the author of both. Reason and empirical observation were given space to explore "things earthly" without fear of overthrowing heaven. It was only when science, after the Enlightenment, attempted to exceed its limits of observation and pontificate on the nature of the unseen that it fell into the same confusion that had been the embarrassment of the Roman Catholic Church. While many Christians were nervous about the rise of astronomy and the potential changes it could bring in the way one understood the universe, Calvin warned, "This study is not to be reprobated, nor is this science to be condemned, because some frantic persons are wont boldly to reject whatever is unknown to them."[6]

The Reformers, therefore, gave a great space to "natural revelation" and the secular disciplines in unfolding divine wisdom in ways that complemented the Scriptures. Since they were convinced that the Bible was about Christ rather than about science, they had no trouble accepting the idea that a great many disturbing and upsetting changes could take place in our understanding of the universe without overthrowing the infallible revelation of Scripture. Perhaps our assumptions about what the Bible teaches could be overthrown, but eventually we would come to see that the new discoveries (if founded on fact) harmonized perfectly with Scripture, no matter how they differed from our own cherished opinions. John Dillenberger observes that the Reformers "were positive about the role of the sciences generally and of astronomy particularly. The theological approach of Luther and Calvin provided a view of Scripture and science which could have been open to Copernicus."[7]

Protestant Scholasticism, the movement immediately following the Reformation, which refined and systematized evangelical Protestantism into a coherent whole, continued this affirming attitude toward science and helped greatly to contribute to its rise. Kepler, Bacon, and Newton are among the brightest stars in this constellation. (Kepler referred to the enterprise as "thinking God's thoughts after him" and was an early supporter of the new Copernican theories.)

The Puritans founded the famous Royal Society, citadel of British sciences. One of its founders, Thomas Sprat, compared the Reformation, with its liberation of the Word of God from human additions, to the rise of the sciences, crediting the former for the latter. Robert Boyle (1627–91), an earlier pioneer of physics, wished the fellows of the Royal Society well in their "laudable attempts to discover the true nature of the works of God, and [prayed] that they and all other searchers into physical truths may cordially refer their attainments to the glory of the Author of Nature and the benefit of mankind."[8] Stanford's Lewis Spitz notes, too, that Boyle wrote a book titled *The Excellency of Theology, Compared with Natural Philosophy,* and Spitz observes, "No one can deny the preponderance of Protestants among scientists after the 1640's. Lutherans, Anglicans, and preeminently Calvinists made more scientific discoveries than Catholics and appeared to be more flexible in putting them to use."[9]

In Education

A final area of concern for the Reformers that we will consider is education, for here we in our day particularly feel the sting of H. G. Wells's remark, "Civilization is a race between education and catastrophe."

The Reformers did not merely curse the darkness; they were determined to work positively for the good of their neighbor and the glory of God.

Martin Luther persuaded the government to mandate compulsory universal education for the first time in Western history, for both girls and boys. With associates he created a system of public education for Germany. Christianity was a religion of the word, and those who were dependent on religious images and hearsay were, first of all, spiritually impoverished. But they were also culturally impoverished, and that was an important point as well. To that end, Luther's sidekick Melanchthon declared, "The ultimate end which confronts us is not private virtue alone but the interest of the public weal," and he exhorted teachers "to take up a school vocation in the same spirit that you would take up the service of God in the church."[10] Imagine the freedom that this gave to the average public school teacher! Calvin argued in his 1541 *Ordinances,* "Since it is necessary to prepare for the coming generations in order not to leave the church a desert for our children, it is imperative that we establish a college to instruct the children and to prepare them for both the ministry and civil government." The Academy, which later became the University of Geneva, became a model for the great universities of Europe and the New World. Many of the names associated with the rebuilding or foundation of the great universities were at one time students of this Academy. In 1536, the citizens of Geneva signed a pact to send their children to the recently opened public schools.

John Comenius was a Polish reformer who sought to integrate his Reformation worldview with the vision of universal public education. He is regarded by many as the father of modern education. Advanced for the time, his educational philosophy revolutionized entire sections of Europe.

Similarly, *The First Book of Discipline,* drawn up by John Knox in 1560, called for a national public education system for Scotland. Former monasteries were turned into libraries and schools. As Lewis Spitz states, "It was no accident that universal literacy was first achieved in Scotland and in several German Protestant states."[11] Far from being anti-intellectual or fearful of secular learning, the Reformers believed that Christianity could only thrive among a literate and educated populace. Their humanistic training had amply prepared them for their task; out of the Reformed tradition alone were born the universities of Zurich, Strasbourg and Geneva, Edinburgh, Leiden, Utrecht, Amsterdam, Harvard, Yale, Princeton, Brown, Dartmouth, and Rutgers. The Puritans restored Oxford and Cambridge, and the German Lutheran and Reformed churches rebuilt the decaying University of Heidelberg. In reaction to this massive educational movement, the Jesuits were founded to build universities and colleges to combat the spread of Protestantism.

"But that was so long ago, and people were interested in learning then," some will say. And yet, Calvin's mentor and chief reformer in Strasbourg, Martin Bucer, lamented,

> Nobody will learn anything nowadays except what brings in money. All the world is running after those trades and occupations which give least work to do and bring the most gain, without any concern for their neighbor or for honest and good report. The study of the arts and sciences is set aside for the basest kinds of manual work. . . . All the clever heads which have been endowed by God with capacity for the nobler studies are engrossed by commerce.[12]

The Reformers did not merely curse the darkness; they were determined to work positively for the good of their neighbor and the glory of God. They took up the standard and raised the standards for an entire age, beyond simply lamenting conditions and proposing legislation. It was far from perfect, but it was a remarkable experiment in what can be done when God's people are liberated by the Gospel for their neighbor's good and their Redeemer's glory.

But this evangelical witness, of course, did not end with the sixteenth and seventeenth centuries, just as it did not begin there.

TODAY

One modern example is Abraham Kuyper (1837–1920), whose career began as a liberal pastor in the Netherlands. After graduating from the University of Leiden with his theology degree, Kuyper was called by a small country parish where a number of his parishioners converted him to orthodox faith in Christ. From then on, he became a popular preacher in Amsterdam as he challenged liberalism with sound arguments, becoming the editor of the daily newspaper, *De Standaard,* and then, adding to his busy life, membership in the Dutch Parliament. Kuyper committed himself to the calling of a statesman and founded the Anti-revolutionary Party, a national system of Christian schools, and the Free University of Amsterdam, where he declared in his inaugural address, "There is not an inch in the entire domain of our human life of which Christ, who is sovereign of all, does not proclaim, 'Mine!'"

Kuyper's dedication to democratic principles did not sit well with many of Kuyper's colleagues, and his commitment to civil rights for workers alienated him from many within his own party. In spite of these odds, Kuyper was given an honorary doctorate from Princeton in 1898 and then became the Prime Minister of The Netherlands three years later. After his official career, Kuyper assumed the role of elder statesman and wrote many books on a variety of subjects about which he seemed to have an encyclopedic knowledge, writing books about art, the railroad, travels, and the impending crisis of cultural authority in the West.

One of Kuyper's important contributions was his insistence that Christians in politics serve the whole nation and that they should not simply advance their own good. "The little people," one of Kuyper's favorite phrases, were in truth the great people whom the magistrate must serve with great diligence. Therefore, Kuyper was capable of entering what had become a pluralistic environment and upholding the liberties of all Dutch citizens and immigrants, while encouraging the advancement of each group by freeing it to pursue its own hopes, language, cultural traditions, and religious faith. It was in this environment that Christianity flourished again in that nation, though not without a good number of problems within the churches themselves.

Nevertheless, Kuyper did make "Christian" versions of many things in the world: Christian schools, newspapers, and political parties tended to obscure the earlier Protestant confidence in the realm of nature as possessing sufficient light and justification for its existence without having to be organized as specifically Christian. This Kuyperian spirit has been especially attractive in some circles in North America, because it is world-embracing and eschews the pietistic retreat from society, and yet it should not be too hastily concluded that one can find a distinctively "Christian" philosophy, political theory, or aesthetic. If these are indeed realms of common grace and natural revelation, they do not require a specifically Christian explanation. Looking for one will only tend to polarize Christians from non-Christians until believers are at last exiled again from the public square, forced to pursue their "Christian" philosophy in their own spiritual ghetto.

There is also a danger in some forms of Kuyperian thought in terms of confusing the lordship of Christ in redemption (i.e., over His church) and the lordship of Christ over creation. If, for instance, an evangelical leader were to stand up this week and declare, in Kuyper's words, "There is not an inch in the entire domain of our human life of which Christ, who is sovereign over all, does not proclaim, 'Mine!'," the secular media would probably take that as an attempt to impose the Christian faith on the whole society. And yet, Kuyper himself was not referring to a religious coup, but underscoring the lordship of Christ over "the entire domain of *our* human life"—in other words, the lives of *believers* are to be regulated and ruled by the revealed will of God, not just on Sunday, but on Monday as well. Every thought must be made captive to Christ, Paul declared. All men and women *should* bow to Christ's rule over all of life, but only believers *will* do this—until the last day, when "every knee should bow, and every tongue confess that Jesus Christ is Lord, to the glory of God the Father" (Philippians 2:10–11). Contemporary religious pluralism renders all the various attempts at "Christendom" anachronistic; however, there is much that remains useful.

By the end of his life, Kuyper had led the way to a national Reformed Church that had recovered its orthodoxy and living faith, he had started a national system of Christian schools, and he had served those beyond the scope of Christianity as their prime minister.

Many others left God's mark on the world. David Livingstone, the great missionary and explorer, worked indefatigably to end the slave trade in Africa, as the British prime minister William Wilberforce and his circle of Christian friends in government finally brought that institution to an end. We see the same impulse in a shy and unassuming Corrie ten Boom and in the lives of countless other Christians of the Dutch resistance who hid Jews in their homes and workshops at the peril of their own lives. When the Japanese officer who launched the attack on Pearl Harbor was converted to Christ, and he embraced the American officer—a Christian—who had been in charge during the attack, this world-embracing spirit was alive and well.

Countless heroes simply carry out their tasks with God's glory and the service of their family and neighbor in view. Many of those to whom I have referred are European, with special reference to the Protestant Reformation, and that is only because it was that movement that recovered many of these insights that can bring a fresh appraisal of our place in this world. This message has made countless men and women in every nation who are small in the eyes of the world great in the kingdom of God. But it has also produced many of the cultural benefits that can make our world a more hospitable place in which to hear the best news of all, the news that makes all of our greatest gains in culture pale by comparison. In the next chapter we'll look at balancing the various spheres in which believers are involved.

NOTES

1. C. Peter Wagner, *Spiritual Power and Church Growth* (Altamonte Springs, Fla.: Strang Communications, 1986), 41–42.

2. Ewald M. Plass, *What Luther Says* (St. Louis: Concordia, 1986), No. 3815.

3. Ibid., No. 474.

4. Cited in Plass, *What Luther Says,* 612 ff.

5. John Calvin, *Commentary on Genesis,* trans. John King (Grand Rapids: Eerdmans, 1948), 85–87.

6. Ibid.

7. John Dillenberger, *Protestant Thought and Natural Science* (Westport, Conn.: Greenwood, 1977).

8. Ibid., 589.

9. Lewis Spitz, *The Renaissance and Reformation Movements* (Chicago: Rand McNally, 1971), 581.

10. Ibid., 558.

11. Ibid.

12. Ibid., 560.

Chapter Two

∎

SPHERE SOVEREIGNTY: MINDING OUR OWN BUSINESS

∎

One more aid to being a worldly Christian is Abraham Kuyper's notion of "sphere sovereignty," which he adapted from the Reformers' insistence upon staying within the sphere of one's calling and making the boundaries clear.

Do we change the schools through politics? Must art serve a moral, political, religious, or therapeutic end other than merely providing aesthetic pleasure and delight? Has sports taken on too great a place in our society? These are just some of the practical questions that can find some usefulness in this principle.

It has come to mean more than this, namely, the distinct existence of every human activity—not only each sphere's independence from the state, but from the other spheres as well. As Kuyper, Meeter, and other advocates of sphere sovereignty argue, this notion is not derived from a dislike of either the state or the church, or for any of the other institutions or cultural tasks. In Scripture, we find the cultural tasks given before the creation of government, the latter being necessitated by the Fall. As they are prior in creation, they are throughout Scripture given a distinct existence, as when Cain's city-building is contrasted with Seth's kingdom-building.

Henry Meeter defines this idea as follows:

> By this is meant that the cultural, philanthropic organizations, and whatever other groups naturally develop out of the organic life of human society, as well as churches, do not owe their origin, existence, or principle of life to the State. They have an inner principle and cultural task all their own, entrusted to them by God. . . . Upon this sovereignty given them by the Creator the State may not infringe.[1]

Unlike many of the caricatures, Protestantism has historically opposed an individualism that views either the church or society merely as a collection of individuals. Many Christians today would approve of the above quote because of their disdain for the government, and many secularists would approve of it because of their dislike for the church, but the basis for this notion is a biblical consideration. A significant discussion in philosophy ever since Heraclitus and Parmenides, the debate over individualism (the many) versus collectivism (the one) has taken on special relevance in the twentieth century, as we have seen both anarchy and totalitarian communism uproot entire races and lead to genocide across Europe and, more recently, in Africa and Asia. Is society merely a collection of isolated selves, each pursuing his or her own interests that happen occasionally to coincide with other isolated selves? This cannot be lightly dismissed as philosophical theorizing, since the answer to that question has moved armies and has had perhaps more to do with the undermining of the family in the modern West than politics or the divorce rate.

We will discuss this idea more fully in the chapter on politics, but here it is important to introduce the subject because it relates to everything else we will discuss. For instance, in politics, Christian activists and secular liberals are often more alike than either would want to admit. They seem to share a dependence upon the state and the political or judicial sphere for solving the moral and spiritual problems in society. According to recent surveys, evangelical Christians are as likely to divorce and abuse children in the home; they contribute their share of abortions to the national catastrophe; and Christian teenagers are actually likely to watch more hours of MTV than their non-Christian counterparts. Evangelical parents may press with angry resolution for prayer and the posting of the Ten Commandments in public schools, but most evangelical Christians cannot name the Ten Commandments themselves and demonstrate an appalling illiteracy with regard to the Bible's most basic themes and facts.

The question arises, therefore, Is it not wiser to focus on the duties of parents in the home than to lay the burden at the door of politicians? Whether it is encouraging financial dependence and a feeling of entitlement for being a minority or encouraging political and judicial solutions to our enormous moral and spiritual crises, Christians and secularists alike seem to be children of their age to a rather significant degree.

In art also we expect there to be some social usefulness for the enterprise. It must aid us in worship or evangelism, or it must encourage morality and civic patriotism or develop character. But art has its own intrinsic worth and value assigned to it by the Creator of all good things. As the Christian art historian H. R. Rookmaker so succinctly stated, "Art needs no justification."

If the state is destitute of family life, or if the church is shallow and corrupt in its ministry, the whole society groans with disease and self-destruction.

Nor is the family an appendage of some other institution. Sometimes, we think of either the state or the church as more important, as when a Christian spends so much time in political activism or church activities that his or her own children become casualties of the very war in which the person is so zealously engaged. In times of great persecution or deep and pervasive secularism, the people of God have always doubled their energies in their family duties: Children are urged to learn the catechism under the tutelage of godly parents who model the uniquely Christian life view and lifestyle by both their teaching and personal example. This does not mean that they become more strict and serious in their personality, but that they become more passionate about the Word of God and its impact on the circle of parishioners closest to them. Therefore, the home becomes a refuge, a "little church," as Luther called it—even a "little seminary," where children at least know enough about what they believe and why they believe it to distinguish them from the unbelieving world. At first, this may be perceived as escapism: Since we cannot win the world, let's retreat into the four walls of our own home. Isn't this, after all, exactly what the secularists want us to do—to keep our faith out of the public square? It does not matter what the secularists want us to do; what matters is what God wants us to do, and He has declared that it is His will that parents assume the full responsibility for their families. They are neither to blame nor to rely on other institutions (the state, the schools, or "the world" in general) for the condition of the home.

The home is so basic and the central of all social institutions not only because it was the first institution of society founded by God, but because it is the nursery of the church. The family, therefore, is the only social institution that is both secular and sacred. An atheistic family is no less founded by God than is a Christian household; it is a creation ordinance. Just as unbelievers and believers alike participate in the divine image, in possessing a divine calling or vocation in the world, and in sharing common grace, so they create families not merely out of a biological instinct, but, due to that divine image, they continue to be creatures who require communion. The familial relationships are the most basic to human nature. Nevertheless, the Christian home is, in Scripture, distinguished sharply from that of unbelievers: "The Lord's curse is on the house of the wicked, but he blesses the home of the righteous" (Proverbs 3:33). The believer's home is the most local expression of the body of Christ, and, therefore, it is both a civil institution, rooted in creation, and a sacred institution, rooted in redemption. Sanctified by water and the Word, this holy assembly is to be zealously guarded and defended by the father, who exercises his priesthood in the home, and by the mother, who also shares in the priesthood of all believers. No institution, not even the church, is to have priority over the home. So seriously did Kuyper take this point that the Christian schools in Holland were organized and supervised by the parents, not by either the government or the church.

But this only worked because the parents were themselves well-taught in their churches, so we see immediately the link between the spheres, while each retains its distinct identity. If the state is destitute of family life, or if the church is shallow and corrupt in its ministry, the whole society groans with disease and self-destruction. The answer is not ultimately to be found in politics, the church, or the home, but in God, as He reforms and rebuilds all three of these distinct institutions, liberating each to pursue its divinely ordained role without confusion with other spheres. A church, then, is set back on track by restoring its confidence in the power of the Word; a family, by restoring its confidence in the importance of both quality leisure time together as well as fellowship in the Scriptures; and a nation, by restoring its *secular* mission—to protect its citizens against foreign or domestic aggression. Only by clearly distinguishing these spheres are we able to have sane and reasonable expectations of the various institutions in which we are commonly involved.

> *By "culture," we mean the tastes*
> *that rule a particular people.*

As we have already seen, Calvin's concern that much of the social confusion in his day was because men and women were transgressing the boundaries of their calling is relevant especially in our day. When ministers become politicians, or politicians invoke God's name in civil religion; when artists become evangelists or preacher-teachers (or politicians); or public education, art, and science become heavily politicized, there is a deep impoverishment of the society. Educators should be concerned with teaching students, not with lobbying Washington; artists should be devoted to their craft, not to making political or religious propaganda; politicians should be dedicated to civil duties, not to saving the nation spiritually, materially, or morally; and we should expect the church to proclaim the Word, administer the sacraments, and maintain good order and discipline among professing Christians, not to confuse its mission with any of these other important, but distinct, spheres of creation.

Given that we need to make distinctions between "things heavenly" and "things earthly," and between "common grace" and "saving grace," as well as between the various spheres of human activity, where do we go from here? Before we get to the practical details, we should lay out our options.

CHRIST AND CULTURE

Published in 1951, *Christ and Culture,* by Yale's H. Richard Niebuhr, for decades reigned as an outline of the distinct approaches to culture taken by the various Roman Catholic and Protestant bodies. As we will see later, there are some problems with Niebuhr's survey, but it is helpful in organizing our thoughts on this important subject.

Never in our nation's history has such a survey been more important, especially given the confusion that we have been discussing. Niebuhr, who was a German Reformed neo-orthodox theologian, classed five different approaches. Let us, then, take each in its turn. But before that, let's attempt to briefly define what is meant by "culture." Derived from the world of gardening (viz., horti*culture, culti*vation of land, etc.), the Germans recruited the word to refer to the cultivation of the habits, interests, language, and artistic life of the nation. By "culture," we mean the tastes that rule a particular people, whether the elites (high culture) or the masses (popular culture). Although there are many subcultures in every culture, there are broad tendencies that mark a people generally, and that is what we intend by "culture" in that which follows.

Christ Against Culture

The first group of Christians to express this approach were the first Christians, and their response is quite understandable. Although Paul counseled early Christians, "Make it your ambition to lead a quiet life, to mind your own business and to work with your hands . . . so that your daily life may win the respect of outsiders and so that you will not be dependent on anybody" (1 Thessalonians 4:11), there was at times intense persecution that accentuated the sense of being strangers and aliens in this world. While some were members of the cultural elite, Paul notes of the Corinthian Christians that they had among them "not many wise, not many of noble birth." The church drew in rich and poor, slave and free, male and female, Jew and Gentile, and those from every strata in society. They were connected to each other because of the Gospel. Although their earthly stations occasionally led to conflict, the Christian hope transcended temporal categories.

It is difficult to have a terribly optimistic view of one's impact on culture when being thrown to lions, and the persecutions intensified the wilderness experience of these first Christians who longed for a better city.

The Latin Father Tertullian expressed the "Christ against culture" sentiment well in his opposition to secular philosophy. "What indeed has Athens to do with Jerusalem?" he demanded. But the Anabaptists of the sixteenth century picked up on this theme again in the crucible of persecution. Deriving their name from the practice of rebaptizing adults, Anabaptists reacted against Rome more sharply than the Reformers, renouncing infant baptism. Furthermore, they never did really embrace the Reformation's central doctrine of justification by grace alone through faith alone. Anabaptism represents a legalistic strain in its doctrine of salvation and the Christian life, along with a sectarian view of the church and its relation to society. In our own day, Anabaptist groups remain, ranging from the more open Mennonites to the more reclusive Amish communities of western Pennsylvania. Radically opposed to involvement in secular affairs, the Anabaptists adopted the position enshrined in their Schleichtheim Confession of Faith:

> We are agreed on separation: A separation shall be made from the evil and from the wickedness which the devil planted in the world; in this manner, simply that we shall not have fellowship with the

wicked and not run with them in the multitude of their abomina-
tions. This is the way it is: Since all who do not walk in the obedience of faith, and have not united themselves with God so that
they wish to do his will, are a great abomination before God, it is
not possible for anything to grow or issue from them except abom-
inable things. For truly all creatures are in but two classes, good
and bad, believing and unbelieving, darkness and light, the world
and those who have come out of the world, God's temple and
idols, Christ and Belial; and none can have part with the other.
. . . God further admonishes us to withdraw from Babylon and the
earthly Egypt that we may not be partakers of the pain and suffering which the Lord will bring upon them.

This shunning of the world includes not only Roman Catholic and Protestant (i.e., Lutheran or Reformed) services, but
"drinking houses, civic affairs," and other secular associations.

From all these things we shall be separated and have no part with
them for they are nothing but an abomination, and they are the
cause of our being hated before Jesus Christ, who has set us free
from the slavery of the flesh and fitted us for the service of God
through the Spirit whom he has given us.[2]

Refusing to serve in the army or in public office, most Anabaptists even separated themselves physically from the City of
Man, establishing spiritual utopias beyond the city limits, just as
medieval monks had left the pressures of secular stations in order to devote themselves entirely to otherworldly affairs. The
Quakers also followed in the Anabaptist rejection of culture.

Essentially, Anabaptist views of Christ and culture were an-
tagonistic. They felt there was little hope of influencing the larger
culture, and they lived simple lives and eschewed secular art,
music, philosophy, education, and pastimes. Consequently, while
the medieval church and Reformation Protestants produced nu-
merous leaders in arts, letters, and sciences, Anabaptists have
historically remained suspicious of culture.

But the rejection of culture is evident not only in mystics,
monks, and martyrs, but also in those who have secularized the
message of Christ into a liberation from the establishment. It is

42

interesting that Niebuhr includes the famous Russian novelist Leo Tolstoy in this tradition. We could also recall Nietzsche, whose nihilistic philosophy pronounced life meaningless, or Marx, who admired the Anabaptists so greatly that the coinage of the former East Germany bore a tribute to them. The 1960s represent a similar rebellion against culture and "high art." Ironically, when Christians attack "cultural elites" and classical art and literature, they are more like sixties radicals than they might wish.

Those who embrace the "Christ against culture" motif tend to glory in the irrational nature of faith, following Tertullian's famous dictum, "I believe because it is absurd." Although the church father has been unfairly misrepresented for his view, there is undoubtedly a certain opposition of nature and grace, secular and sacred, reason and faith, in this way of thinking. Niebuhr argues that this approach is marked by legalism and "concentration on one's own will rather than on the gracious work of God." There is a suspicion of the natural world, and the Spirit who is directly at work in their hearts is often more prominent than the work of the Father and the Son in redemption. Consequently, Scripture is often secondary to intuitive spiritual hunches, and there is a certain nervousness about saying that God only speaks through ink and paper, water, and bread and wine. These are too earthly, too material. The gnostic element in this approach becomes evident. The world is evil, but the realm of the Spirit is good; earthly things are inherently sinful, while heavenly things are inherently virtuous.

The Christ of Culture

On the other end of the spectrum are those who so identify Christ with a particular culture that He simply exists as the embodiment of one's own culture. As Niebuhr points out, this is the inheritance of Protestant liberalism, with its "culture-Protestantism."

In the noble interest of apologetics and evangelism, German liberalism attempted to make Christianity reasonable to Enlightenment men and women who could no longer believe in miracles. Therefore, Christ was less the God-Man who came to save the world from sin than the Ideal German poet, moralist, or philosopher. He gave His blessing to German pride, and religion was primarily a matter of the soul. Therefore, Jesus saved the soul but left the body to do whatever it willed. We are painfully aware of where this ideology finally led. The evangelical church of Germany actually changed its name to the Reich's Church, and the clergy swore an oath of allegiance to Hitler. A great many Protestant liberal theologians were among the architects of "*Deutchland Uber Alles*" (Germany Over All).

Similarly, in America we run the risk of confusing the nation with Christ. Some politicized evangelicals read the New Testament as if Jesus came from heaven with the express mission to bless America and launch free-market capitalism. Just as mainline liberals in the sixties made Jesus a mascot for left-wing ideology, conservative evangelicals risk the same confusion on the other side of the political spectrum. Niebuhr offers the following judgment of fundamentalism:

> How often the Fundamentalist attack on so-called liberalism—by which cultural Protestantism is meant—is itself an expression of a cultural loyalty, a number of Fundamentalist interests indicate. . . . The mores they associate with Christ have at least as little relation to the New Testament and as much connection with social custom as have those of their opponents. The movement that identifies obedience to Jesus Christ with the practices of prohibition, and with the maintenance of early American social organization, is a type of cultural Christianity; though the culture it seeks to conserve differs from that which its rivals honor. . . . In so far as the contemporary attack on Culture-Protestantism is carried on in this way, it is a family quarrel between folk who are in essential agreement on the main point; namely, that Christ is the Christ of culture, and that man's greatest task is to maintain his best culture. Nothing in the Christian movement is so similar to cultural Protestantism as cultural Catholicism, nothing more akin to German Christianity than American Christianity. . . . Christ is identified with what men conceive to be their finest ideals, their noblest institutions, and their best philosophy.[3]

In American evangelicalism, cultural Christianity has produced an unusual confidence in the ability of the American spirit to accomplish whatever is necessary. "Christ" is an idea more than a person, a guarantor of basic American values and assumptions. Therefore, says Niebuhr, "Cultural Christianity, in modern times at least, has always given birth to movements that tended toward the extreme of self-reliant humanism, which found the doctrine of grace—and even more the reliance upon it—demeaning to man and discouraging to his will." This is why Arminianism works so well in America and Calvinism is so disdained. Calvinism can never serve the idealistic or optimistic individualist who believes that there is something unique in the national character that predisposes a sinner to become a saint by hard work. In Reformation theology, God judges and justifies; in Arminianism, man decides and pulls himself up by the bootstraps.

Christ Above Culture

This category is more nuanced than the preceding two, as it suggests neither antagonism nor assimilation. In this approach, says Niebuhr, "the fundamental issue does not lie between Christ and the world, important as that issue is, but between God and man." In other words, it views this whole question in more of a vertical (God to man) than a horizontal (Christ and culture) direction.

According to its proponents, this view suggests that the world is neither to be cursed nor blessed. Upheld by a gracious God, it is nevertheless in opposition to God. There is an attempt to synthesize Christ and culture, but not to simply "baptize" one's own culture with Christianity. This is the position Niebuhr attributes to Thomas Aquinas.

Christ and Culture in Paradox

Our fourth option Niebuhr refers to as "dualism" because it rejects the attempts of the "Christ above culture" types to synthesize these two spheres. Instead, this position affirms the "dual citizenship" of every Christian who is a member of the City of God and the City of Man simultaneously. Neither sphere is to rule the other, nor is either sphere to attack the other. They are simply different spheres with different purposes.

Those who embrace this view are most likely to emphasize God's grace. Grace is in God; sin is in man. Adherents of this position will not seek to locate God's grace in culture or in oneself, but they clearly distinguish creation and redemption. Lutherans are the most ardent defenders of "Christ and culture in paradox," according to Niebuhr's scheme. Culture can never be an avenue of finding God, and here the opposition to "Christ of culture" is evident. But neither can culture be an object of disgust, since culture never promises to save or redeem. It exists for a distinct purpose, and when a man or woman finds pleasure in work, family life, education, arts, or leisure, it is a gift of God, but not a redemptive gift.

Calvin urged believers to so live by the light of special revelation (the Bible) that their influence could be detected in the wider culture.

Luther emphasized this theme with his doctrine of the "two kingdoms." The worldly left hand holds the sword of earthly power, while the heavenly right hand holds the sword of the Spirit, the Word of God. One cannot attempt to coerce faith, nor can one attempt to accommodate faith to secular modes of thought. Luther recovered Augustine's emphasis on the "two cities," and Calvin buttressed it with his own defense of the two kingdoms, especially in *The Institutes.*

> Therefore, in order that none of us may stumble on that stone [of confusing Christ and culture], let us first consider that there is a twofold government in man: . . . The one we may call the spiritual kingdom, the other, the political kingdom. Now these two, as we have divided them, must always be examined separately; and while one is being considered, we must call away and turn aside the mind from thinking about the other. There are in man, so to speak, two worlds, over which different kings and different laws have authority. (3.19.15)

It is for this reason, Calvin says, that the moral law of God written on the human conscience is sufficient for framing a just society. In other words, it need not be an explicitly Christian society in order to be just and full of civil virtues:

> It is a fact that the law of God which we call the moral law is nothing else than a testimony of natural law and of that conscience which God has engraved upon the minds of men. . . . Hence, this equity alone must be the goal and rule and limit of all laws. Whatever laws shall be framed to that rule, directed to that goal, bound by that limit, there is no reason why we should disapprove of them, howsoever they may differ from the Jewish [Old Testament civil] laws, or among themselves.

Calvin insisted that, according to the biblical text itself, God had taken Israel into a special theocratic relationship and therefore "had special concern for it in making its laws." The nations, being "common" instead of "holy," are ruled by general revelation (the law written on the conscience) rather than by special revelation (Scripture). He thought that the Anabaptist groups that wished to impose the civil laws of the Old Testament were "malicious and hateful toward public welfare." "For the Lord through the hand of Moses did not give that law to be proclaimed among all nations and to be in force everywhere" (*Institutes*, 4.20.14–16).

And yet, Calvin urged believers to so live by the light of special revelation (the Bible) that their influence could be detected in the wider culture. This brings us to the next model.

Christ the Transformer of Culture

The final classification in Niebuhr is also the one he particularly favors. "Though they hold fast to the radical distinction between God's work in Christ and man's work in culture, they do not take the road of exclusive Christianity into isolation from civilization, or reject its institutions with Tolstoyan bitterness." Proponents of this view suffer under no illusions that this world will ever be transformed into Paradise by human progress, but they are also eager to see God's hand in the advances in science, medicine, the arts, and learning in general. Nor do they wish merely to stand on the sidelines, watching God's providential arm at work; they want to be His agents of reform in the world around them.

The sovereignty of God plays a large role in this approach. Although it may be too critical to charge the Anabaptist with not really trusting God's sovereign intervention in worldly affairs, it is clear that he or she does not intend to be a vessel in this enterprise. But "transformational Christians" do not simply want to "baptize" the worldly establishment either. They want to change it for the better. By wanting to change it, they affirm that culture is not as it should be, while also affirming that they believe that culture still, in all of its fallenness, remains a place of divine concern and activity. "Their more affirmative stand," writes Niebuhr, "seems to be closely connected with three theological convictions." These are: (1) The importance of the doctrine of creation. Other Christians may focus so much on redemption that they fail to appreciate the fact that even in its fallenness, the world is, as Calvin put it, "a theater of God's glory." The non-Christian still bears God's image and, by common grace, is capable of great feats of cultural good. (2) The conviction that humanity is fallen. Like the dualist, the transformer affirms total depravity, but he is anxious to distinguish this from an ontological or essential evil. In other words, he wants to correct the misunderstanding that we are sinful because we are human or because we have material bodies. The transformer emphasizes sin as a consequence of moral rebellion. It is man's fault, not God's, and it is—again in Calvin's words—"the corruption of nature, not nature itself" that is to blame. Therefore, the problem is not the world, but the willful opposition of the world to God and His Christ. This frees the believer to participate in the world as a full-fledged citizen and to view it not as inherently wicked, but as the theater in which both God's glory and human sin are displayed. (3) The transformer also believes that the world is awaiting complete redemption (Romans 8:19–23).

The transformer acknowledges, with the dualist and the Anabaptist, that evil will never be fully or even significantly conquered this side of Christ's return, but he is more expectant of partial victories from time to time. For the transformer, it is not as if time is set against eternity, or this world is set in opposition to the next, but neither is it that the two worlds simply collapse into each other. There are two distinct spheres, but God is active in both. Therefore, for the transformer, it is not enough to simply care for the soul; the entire life of humanity is in view. God is both creator and redeemer, and He redeems not only individual souls, but "makes all things new." The transformer neither worships culture nor hates it; he neither expects final victory in this life nor final ruin. This view is advanced by St. Augustine, John Calvin, and the Reformed tradition.

SCRIPTURE AND CULTURE

Earlier, I mentioned that Niebuhr's work, although a landmark in 1951, possesses some weaknesses. First, it has a tendency toward reductionism. It is too simplistic to plug various movements or individuals into tidy categories. For instance, the Roman church represented diverse movements. The monks followed either a "Christ against culture" or a "Christ above culture" motif, while the popes followed more of a "Christ of culture" approach, viewing Christianity and "Christendom"—that is, European culture—as one and the same. Similarly, neither Augustine nor Calvin can be seen merely as "transformer" types, since they provided the front end and back end, respectively, of Luther's "dualist" interpretation. No one anticipates Luther's "two kingdoms" more clearly than Augustine, and no one elucidates and builds on that foundation more rigorously than John Calvin.

Nevertheless, the categories do allow us to gain a broad grid through which to view the different options available to us. But the real question in deciding our approach is, "What do the Scriptures teach?"

Throughout the Old Testament, we learn that there are two kingdoms: the City of God and the City of Man. In the earthly "theocracy," Israel is a spiritual nation—in other words, God's rule and culture are united as the nation mirrors the kingdom of God (and, in fact, *is* the kingdom of God). But when Israel violated the covenant, she was exiled from the land of promise, and the two kingdoms were once again divided. The people of God still existed, but in exile from the land of God.

In the New Covenant, God's people are no longer tied to a physical plot of land, but are heirs of the heavenly kingdom (see especially Hebrews 4 and 11). Throughout the New Testament, ever since our Lord's announcement to Pilate that "now my kingdom is from another place" (John 18:36), believers have set their hopes on "a better country—a heavenly one. Therefore God is not ashamed to be called their God, for he has prepared a city for them" (Hebrews 11:16). This is what our Lord meant when He declared, "I am going there to prepare a place for you" (John 14:2).

Scripture admonishes us, therefore, to avoid either the tendency to confuse the kingdom of God with an earthly nation (Israel, America, etc.) or, on the other hand, to view citizenship in one kingdom as completely antithetical to citizenship and participation in the other.

Allow me to conclude, then, with some brief applications. In our day, we are faced, as Niebuhr himself observed, with an evangelicalism that exhibits both a "Christ against culture" and a "Christ of culture" temperament. Why would two conflicting theories guide our involvement? For a number of reasons. First, we are doctrinally adrift. We often leap into action before we connect our involvement to well-conceived theological convictions. And because we are theologically confused—not sure, for instance, whether the world is God's or the devil's, or why, and not quite certain what we should expect in a fallen world—our action is often schizophrenic. On one hand, we share with the Anabaptists a hatred for high culture, yet, with the Protestant liberals, we share an addiction to popular culture. At least part of the "culture wars" waged in the name of Christ is more the result of middle-class suspicion of well-educated, artistic, literary tastes than a struggle for spiritual values. To say that we disdain "high culture" is not to say that we disdain culture in every sense. We ape the secular culture in our fascination with success, fashion, popularity, the noisy, the spectacular, and the vanity of a television society. We are at least as formed (or deformed) by modern technology as by Scripture, and we rarely notice the worldliness of popular culture, even while we attack the "cultural elite." We smell worldliness at Harvard, but swallow it whole in some Christian books and in much of contemporary Christian music.

There is a great danger in mixing a "Christ against culture" and a "Christ of culture" paradigm. When we despise culture, but are nevertheless very active—at least on a political level—in that culture, our interaction comes off as strident, harsh, and angry. We do not come off as those who are interested in transforming culture, but as those who, like some of the revolutionary German Anabaptists who overthrew the city of Munster, want to destroy culture in order to establish an earthly Paradise. When combined with a "Christ of culture" approach, this mixture leads us to simply replace one culture with another and confuse the latter with God's will and kingdom.

The proposal I think our forebears would offer us is to adopt a position roughly equivalent to a combination of the "Christ and culture in paradox" and the "Christ the transformer of culture" paradigms. Adherents of both positions need each other, because this is my Father's world, and yet, this world is not my home.

What are the practical implications of this way of thinking? In the next chapter we will explore the matter of reading secular literature and studying secular wisdom, especially in the light of Paul's warning against "vain philosophies."

NOTES

1. H. Henry Meeter, *The Basic Ideas of Calvinism* (Grand Rapids: Guardian, 1975), 157.
2. Mark Noll, ed., *Confessions and Catechisms of the Reformation* (Grand Rapids: Baker, 1991), 53.
3. All citations from Niebuhr are taken from *Christ and Culture* (New York: Harper, 1951).

Chapter Three

∎

"VAIN PHILOSOPHY": A COP-OUT FOR ANTI-INTELLECTUALISM?

∎

S ee to it that no one takes you captive through hollow and deceptive philosophy." (Colossians 2:8).

Elizabeth was a bright young Christian with a keen interest in learning. Having been recently converted, she was eager to serve the Lord. When she was led to the Scriptures by her new Christian friends, she was delighted to learn everything she could. But Elizabeth's zealous friends grew increasingly worried about her attentive and persistent study of "secular philosophy" —the wisdom of the world. Eventually, Elizabeth was faced with a fork in the road: whether to continue with Christ or investigate the ideas of mere mortals. After months of reluctant, but gradual, distance, she had at last so filled her days with Bible study, prayer, evangelism, and fellowship on campus that she forgot the pain of leaving Aristotle's subtle discussions in the shadows of her worldly past.

Often, setting aside "worldly wisdom" occurs alongside the burning of secular record albums, and Elizabeth's story doubtless finds empathetic readers among those working through this volume.

But this tension is not new by any means. "It is philosophy that supplies the heresies with their equipment," declared the great second-century African father Tertullian. Facing such ominous threats as Gnosticism, which attempted to blend elements of Christianity, Judaism, and Greek philosophy, Tertullian snapped, "A plague on Aristotle, who taught them dialectic, the art which destroys as much as it builds." A method of framing an argument, "dialectic" is the most common form of classical debate, leading off with a major premise (Dogs chase cats), followed by a minor premise (But my pet is a cat), leading to a conclusion (Therefore, my pet will be chased by dogs). As Aristotle himself pointed out, an argument may be *valid*—that is, its conclusion may follow very logically and incontrovertibly from its premises, but the real question one must ask after all of that work is, Are my premises *correct?* Ever since this method of dialogue captured the Athenean Academy, it has been used and misused by good and bad alike, and many from the latter category found great comfort in turning themselves into intellectual pretzels with this dialectical method, so that someone could justify almost any conclusion with a coherent argument, regardless of the truth of the premises.

Tertullian was reacting against the exploitation of this method by the gnostic sect. Their misuse led the church father to dismiss the enterprise entirely from Christian reflection. He appealed to a text that has since been much used (or perhaps abused), where Paul warns the Colossians, "See to it that no one takes you captive through hollow and deceptive philosophy, which depends on human tradition and the basic principles of this world rather than on Christ" (Colossians 2:8; see also 1 Timothy 1:4; 2 Timothy 2:17). After all, Tertullian thundered, "What has Jerusalem to do with Athens, the Church with the Academy, the Christian with the heretic?" And why did he ask that? "After Jesus Christ we have no need of speculation, after the Gospel no need of research. When we come to believe, we have no desire to believe anything else; for we begin by believing that there is nothing else which we have to believe."[1]

On the other hand, there was Tertullian's contemporary, Justin Martyr, who sought to prove Christianity's intellectual and philosophical superiority. Dressed in a philosopher's gown, he opened Rome's first Christian school. He addressed the Roman emperor Hadrian as "the Philosopher, . . . a lover of culture," and proceeded in his "plea for a fair hearing" by demanding that "Reason requires that those who are truly pious and philosophers should honor and cherish the truth alone, scorning merely to follow the opinions of even the ancients, if they are worthless." Following a line of argumentation and evidence for Christianity's truth, Martyr rested the case finally on the reliability of the witnesses to Christ's resurrection and the fulfilled prophecies. In spite of his laudable apologetic approach, just as Tertullian's love for Scripture blinded him to God's common grace among the pagans, so Justin's appreciation for reason often led him to naively embrace secular ideas that undermined the biblical teachings on sin and grace, the nature of the soul, and creation.

The famous paraphrase of Augustine's dictum, "All truth is God's truth," nevertheless kept Augustine from falling into the trap of confusing the Gospel with secular wisdom. And yet, this African bishop of Hippo was himself never entirely rid of the influences of his earlier immersion in Neoplatonic philosophy and Manichaean heresies. It is a difficult tightrope to walk.

At the time of the Reformation, Luther and the other Reformers accused the Roman Catholic Church of having distorted the Gospel with pagan philosophy, whether through the classical rationalism of Plato, the empiricism of Aristotle, or the relativistic penchant for "reconciling" opposites as in the medieval Nicholas of Cusa (fifteenth century). Instead of studying clear biblical passages in order to discover the nature of God, humans, redemption, the church and sacraments, theologians were employing philosophical speculation. The Reformers, therefore, lashed out against confusing spiritual and earthly wisdom just as Paul had—not because they believed reason to be ungodly, but because they believed it had no place in determining the shape of "things heavenly." Only a theology that is *revealed* by God and anchored in Scripture, not in philosophical speculation, could plumb the depths of the divine attributes, human nature, the person and work of Christ, the application of redemption by the Holy Spirit, the nature of the church and the sacraments, and the meaning of history. In fact, the Reformers referred to their contemporaries who wished to extricate themselves from clear biblical passages through a tortuous exercise in philosophical speculation as "sophists," after the ancient Greek philosophical school that advocated a relativistic approach to truth. It is not the truth itself, but the rhetorical brilliance of the one who presents a particular proposition (which he may or may not himself hold), the Sophists held, much like many philosophers in our own day.

In each period of great confusion and unfaithfulness on the part of the church, worldly wisdom has been given the upper hand in shaping the church's views of God, humanity, the world, history, and every other aspect of faith and life. No one ever stands up, waves a flag, and shouts, "We're allowing the world instead of the Word to determine what we believe and how we live," and yet that is exactly what happens in every period of decline. Karl Barth, in our own century, reacted so strongly against a Protestant liberalism that had reduced Christianity to a type of human behavior to be compared to other religions that he insisted that there was no such thing as natural revelation. Fallen and finite human creatures do not find God by their clever speculation; God only reveals Himself in the living and written Word, he declared. To Emil Brunner's defense of natural theology (i.e., the study of that which can be known about God apart from Scripture, which seems to be sanctioned by Romans 1 and 2), Barth thundered back his famous, "Nein!" If Barth and Tertullian are correct, and an openness to philosophy in religion always ends up perverting both, why don't we simply plant our fingers in our ears, ignore the world, and read only the Bible? In fact, a number of us of late have been arguing that secular psychological, marketing, political, and sociological ideologies rule our anti-theological church. So why do we even waste our time with worldly wisdom, if the risk is so great? There are plenty of reasons to risk it, and here I will mention only a few.

THE VALUE OF CREATION

The Bible's warning is against confusing "things heavenly" with "things earthly," not against "things earthly" in general.

When Paul warned, "See to it that no one takes you captive through hollow and deceptive philosophy, which depends on human tradition and the basic principles of this world rather than on Christ" (Colossians 2:8), he was not arguing in Tertullian-like fashion that Christians should regard all human wisdom and philosophy as hostile to the faith. Remember, Paul is the man who argued so eloquently for Christianity from human philosophy in Acts 17. But Paul warned the Colossians against being so earthly-minded that their interests and affections were not driven by the heavenly, eternal, and transcendent. In other words, secular presuppositions continued to guide their worldview when they should be driven by theological, biblical convictions. Like Tertullian, Paul was wrestling with the advocates of Gnosticism—those who blended Christianity and Greek philosophy. The result was a speculative mysticism. Instead of seeing Christianity as an announcement of something that happened (viz., the death and resurrection of Christ), with implications for the whole world, it was a "philosophy of life" that sought primarily to guide one toward a happier and more fulfilling life here and now. Gnosticism, as we have already seen, had a worldview and system of belief that was diametrically opposed to the revealed truth of Scripture: Evil was attributed to matter; salvation was redemption from matter, the world, time, and the body. And this redemption came by following the secret teachings of Jesus and other masters who had learned to deny their physical existence in order to elevate their spirits and achieve unity with the divine.

*The danger is in confusing that
which is to always be distinguished.*

If the Greek mysticism and dualism that provided the foundation for philosophical reflection in the ancient world had been incorporated into Christianity, the biblical view of human nature, the problem of evil, the creation, the fall, and redemption would be distorted beyond recognition.

Therefore, it was not the case that Paul believed that Plato and Aristotle had nothing to say of any truth, relevance, or value, but that whenever they addressed a subject that the Bible addressed, it was always going to be the clear teaching of Scripture, and not philosophical speculation, that would rule the Christian's heart and mind. Philosophers cannot, in other words, speculate their way into God's presence, figuring Him out by their own clever insights. Their sharp logic and brilliant dialectic, vital in the academic enterprise (yes, even in theology), must never take the place of Scripture in telling us about God, ourselves, and the plan of redemption. Scripture must always be the norm, although the most rigorous logical and rational methods may be used in understanding and explaining the text.

But what is interesting in our day is this: Where Tertullian and more moderate church fathers, such as Irenaeus, as well as the Reformers of the sixteenth century, struggled against the tendency to allow philosophy to have more say than theology in the church, today we are struggling against the offspring of that philosophy born in the modern age. Where many evangelicals would insist that they are immune to the "secular, worldly philosophies of men" simply because they have never read much in the way of secular philosophers, the movement itself displays an enormous debt to the philosophical pragmatism of William James, the utilitarianism of John Stuart Mill, and the consumerism of the late twentieth century. Our pastors may not actually read these authors, but they do read church-growth experts who are trained in sociology, psychology, and marketing and often display a greater knowledge of these secular disciplines than of the theology of Scripture.

Recently, a pastor of a conservative evangelical church said that he had to change the name of a sermon series from "Church Doctrines" to "Church Teachings" because few were willing to come to a series with the word "doctrine" in it. Pastors may not actually read Freud, Jung, Rogers, or more recent psychologists, but sermons are being increasingly transformed from theological ("God's Wrath and God's Provision") to therapeutic ("How to Be

Happy and Fulfilled") categories. Sin is "dysfunction" and "sickness," not a condition of spiritual death, hostility toward God, and a complete inability to respond to God (Ephesians 2:1–8; 1 Corinthians 2:12–14; John 1:12–13; 6:44, etc.). Therefore, redemption is "recovery" or one of many versions of "self-help" in the popular market today. Ironically, therefore, those who are often the most self-assured about their immunity to "worldliness" are often the most worldly in real terms, despite their pride in avoiding "secular learning."

Just as Paul appealed to pagan authors on Mars Hill, many of the church fathers found useful wisdom in secular philosophers, and the Reformers and Puritans appreciated their broad learning in pagan as well as biblical literature, so we must recognize that the danger is in *confusing* that which is to always be distinguished. The problem is not with secular literature, but with allowing secular wisdom priority in defining theological beliefs and the spiritual diet of Christian reflection. In fact, secular wisdom is most dangerous not when it comes in a very clearly marked package (i.e., *The Works of Plato, The Writings of Nietzsche, An Introduction to Modern Existentialism,* etc.), but when we naively baptize secular wisdom that we have received second- or third-hand with Bible verses in an effort to be "relevant."

Earthly Problems

Confusing things heavenly and earthly trivializes things earthly.

This confusion of things heavenly and things earthly is a dangerous business. First, it trivializes the problems of this world. When people, for instance, say without compassion that Jesus is the answer to racism, drugs, abortion, depression, and broken homes, while these crises persist very often within conservative Christian as well as non-Christian circles, the first thing it does is trivialize the problems. After all, sin is a complicated thing and even Christians are sinful. We have, since the Fall, tangled ourselves up in a web of deceit, exploitation, manipulation, and willful neglect. As a race and as individuals, we have created a situation in which the path of sin is impossible to trace through every complicated turn. Some problems created by this sinful condition can be treated by the new life of individual Christians and their influence, but since believers are sinful, too, the answers cannot always be that black-and-white. Complicated problems don't succumb to easy answers. Furthermore, the Bible itself is not the answer to everything. It is not a directory for every problem in our lives, for that it is not its author's intention. Addressing us in the form of proclamation, the Bible is specifically directed to the mind, heart, and conscience—bringing home the seriousness of God's judgment and the surprising announcement of God's pardon and justification of the wicked in Christ Jesus. For a generation looking for easy answers to everyday problems that used to be tackled with a phone call to a wise uncle, the Bible loses the seriousness and immensity of its address, drowned in a sea of practicality. If we are to distinguish things heavenly and things earthly, we will have to recognize that the Bible is limited in its scope and interest primarily to ultimate issues. By answering every problem with a Bible verse (usually from Proverbs), we often offer damp solace to souls drenched with despair. Many of these folks, if unaware of the richness and depth of such passages when taken in context, will conclude that the Bible is not adequate for comforting them even in the larger dilemmas of eternity.

> *Instead of meeting God where He allows*
> *Himself to be known (in revelation)*
> *through faith, we try to bring Him down*
> *to us (in experience) through speculation.*

Those who confuse things heavenly and things earthly also trivialize things earthly by assuming that, because of the Fall, there is nothing (or very little) that is true, good, or beautiful in the world that is not specifically Christian. Thus, we have the subculture of "Christian" books, music, art, and paraphernalia. We even have "Christian" entertainment, politicians, cruises, and so on. But this confusion was felt during the Middle Ages also, before the Reformation distinguished and returned dignity to these two spheres. Note Calvin's remarks in this regard, against the "fanatics" who thought secular pursuits "unspiritual" and, therefore, unnecessary:

> Shall we deny that the truth shone upon the ancient jurists who established civic order and discipline with such great equity? Shall we say that the philosophers were blind in their fine observation and artful description of nature? Shall we say that those men were devoid of understanding who conceived the art of disputation and taught us to speak reasonably? Shall we say that they are insane who developed medicine, devoting their labor to our benefit? . . . No, we cannot read the writings of the ancients on these subjects without great admiration. We marvel at them because we are compelled to recognize how eminent they are.
>
> But shall we count anything praiseworthy or noble without recognizing at the same time that it comes from God? Let us be ashamed of such ingratitude, into which not even the pagan poets fell, for they confessed that the gods had invented philosophy, laws, and all useful arts. Those men whom Scripture calls "natural men" were, indeed, sharp and penetrating in their investigation of inferior things. Let us, accordingly, learn by their example how many gifts the Lord left to human nature even after it was despoiled of its true good.[2]

Heavenly Hopes

This confusion of things heavenly and earthly also trivializes things heavenly. This is achieved when pious Christians attempt to make God relevant. Heaven is too high, so instead of meeting God where He allows Himself to be known (in revelation) through faith, we try to bring Him down to us (in experience) through speculation. In other words, sermons on God's attributes, the saving work in Christ, the atonement and justification, sanctification and the sacraments—these are all "up there," removed from the "practical" realm of daily living. Therefore, things heavenly are pulled down into things earthly. The result is a message that is neither earthly enough to be on time and on the cutting edge, nor heavenly enough to say anything really profound and otherworldly in a confused and wayward place.

If we don't think that pagans have anything meaningful to say or contribute to our lives, we will ignore some wonderful gifts of God, and we will also end up trivializing both realms by requiring that things earthly be more than what they should be and that things heavenly should be less.

I think I can make this point with the following analogy. Both the Christian and non-Christian agree with the empirically demonstrable doctrine of death. They differ in their interpretations of its origin, meaning, and solution, but they agree that death happens. It is a reality of human experience. A non-Christian may actually assist a believer in coping with death to a certain extent. For instance, a non-Christian psychologist or medical doctor may write a book explaining how to make a loved one's last days less painful. Does this mean that the Bible is not sufficient in all circumstances, especially in this event of deepest theological significance? Not at all, because the Bible answers the question from a different angle. To say that the Bible is not sufficient for curing diabetes (one thinks of the parents who refused to put their child on insulin because the Bible says "the prayer of faith shall save the sick") is not to say that it is *deficient*. The Bible is sufficient for everything necessary for salvation and godliness. It is, in other words, sufficient for everything pertaining to the scope of its purpose. But the Bible is not a magical catalogue of "how-to" advice or secret formulas for life.

If I were dying of cancer, I would want my pastor to comfort me with the active and passive obedience of Christ, assuring me that in spite of my sinfulness and shortcomings in sanctification, God had accepted me completely in Christ. I would not look for such comfort in worldly wisdom, such as appeals to self-esteem or sentimental (if wholly unfounded) platitudes about "going to a better place," since I realize that an unbelieving author who does not understand sin and grace is not qualified to comfort the soul of a dying Christian. Nevertheless, I would be delighted to learn of practical ideas for making the last days comfortable in other ways that are not addressed by Scripture. Medical procedures calculated to extend my life or ease the pain, dealing with some of the psychological aspects of death and dying, and being reminded of some of the practical relational considerations involved could be of enormous assistance. That book could be very helpful, so long as I knew what I was looking for in it. But too often, "Christian" versions of such books simply confuse the ultimate and proximate issues, attempting to accomplish both tasks by tacking Bible verses, out of context, to every practical problem. The reader often reflects on how lucky he or she is to have found a "safe" book on the subject, avoiding the wisdom of the world.

A person faced with such a situation, therefore, could look for a good, sturdy piece of theology that some who have never read such a thing might regard as impractical. Horatius Bonar's little classic *How Shall I Go to God?* or Thomas Hooker's *The Poor Doubting Christian* would be of much greater comfort to the soul than many contemporary Christian books that attempt to integrate the Bible and psychology or more ostensibly practical ideas. But then it might be good to also pick up that book by the secular author as well, in order to explore some ideas that are beyond the purview of theology. We do not have to justify reading secular literature any more than we have to justify reading theology; it is when we confuse the two that we run into problems. If we knew God's Word well enough to recognize, for instance, that the therapeutic answer, "self-esteem," falls far short of the richness of "There is therefore now no condemnation to those who are in Christ Jesus," we would be capable of discerning the wheat of truth from the chaff of popular sentiment.

A final note on this little illustration should suffice. Christian or not, the terminal illness is just that—terminal—and it ends in death for both individuals. The books by Bonar and Hooker, for example, would be comforting because they are dealing with the *ultimate issues,* which require a divine perspective (i.e., derived from special revelation), not merely dealing with important but *proximate issues,* which simply require expertise or wisdom in a particular field (i.e., derived from general revelation). Once we understand the limitations of both (Scripture limited by God's design for it, and reason limited by both our finitude and sinfulness), we are able to derive comfort and benefit without being disillusioned by expecting more than either is willing or able to deliver.

TAKING EVERY THOUGHT CAPTIVE

When Paul warns, therefore, about being deceived by vain philosophy, he has a particular problem in mind: this confusion of Christianity with Greek philosophy, the latter of which was allowed to intrude carelessly on the former to the extent that the definitions of God, creation, human nature, history, and redemption had been totally recast. Paul was not attacking philosophy per se, but Gnosticism in particular and the domination of theology by secular wisdom in general. That is precisely the problem we see in evangelicalism today, where, for instance, secular notions of the self are imported from pop-psychology (which, ironically, has many affinities to Gnosticism).

But the same apostle who warns against the incursions of philosophy also calls upon the Corinthian believers to encounter it: "We demolish arguments and every pretension that sets itself up against the knowledge of God, and we take captive every thought to make it obedient to Christ" (2 Corinthians 10:5). How can one demolish arguments if one is (a) unfamiliar with the arguments in the first place, (b) uninterested in the merit of those arguments, and (c) incapable of refuting them?

Paul's picture in this passage is crystal clear: It is the image of a soldier who, not content to be on the defensive, is actively pursuing his challengers. Not waiting to be ambushed and taken prisoner, or stationed safely behind the lines, the Christian is anxious to take his enemy captive. We always have to be careful with these images, however, in our day of "culture warring." The enemy is not the unbeliever or worldly institutions, but any and every idea or argument that has the audacious temerity to claim Christ's throne in dictating what we should believe about God, ourselves, redemption, and the meaning of life. The Reformers followed Paul in their love of learning, culture, art, philosophy, and literature. In fact, they and their heirs founded some of the greatest centers of learning in the Western world and encouraged a revival of the humanities (history, philosophy, languages, the arts). Nevertheless, when it came to defining the core matters which the Bible clearly addressed, there human wisdom was deemed insufficient to penetrate the heavenly chamber.

From Genesis to Revelation, the Bible appeals to the intellect and heart as one. Unlike the Greek view, in which the mind and heart are split, the biblical perspective is that the heart is the seat of the intellect. This does not mean that the emotions have a priority over the intellect, but rather it is to suggest that there is an integration of both in the biblical portrait of human existence. After all, the fear of the Lord (an emotional response) may be the beginning of wisdom, but it is the communication of certain facts about God and His activity that induce one to fear and love Him, as the Psalms so powerfully exhibit: "My heart is stirred by a noble theme" (Psalm 45:1). In fact, to the Jewish ear, "the fear of the Lord" would not refer specifically to the emotions any more than to the intellect, as "fear" and "knowledge" were related concepts. We must know something before it can be experienced and lived out in the real world of daily practice.

The Christian witness cannot be naive.
It cannot simply ridicule unbelief.

It is after the recitation of God's saving work in Christ (predestination, calling, justification, glorification) that Paul leaps to his feet in praise: "What shall we say in response to this?" In order to respond, either emotionally or in active and cheerful obedience, we must have something meaningful that elicits that response.

APOLOGETICS

Too often, well-meaning brothers and sisters walk into the middle of the skirmish, anxious to meet their enemy, only to be taken themselves or to be slaughtered before cheerful onlookers. That is why we are told, "Always be prepared to give an answer to everyone who asks you to give the reason for the hope that you have," albeit, "with gentleness and respect" toward the inquirer (1 Peter 3:15). The accent there is on being prepared.

When Paul walked into the Areopagus to present the Christian claims, in Acts 17, he did not go in with a set of reductionistic arguments or references to his own personal testimony of what God had done for him. Nor did he ignore their context. Citing by memory the poetry and prose of secular Greek philosophers, Paul built bridges of understanding. He did this not by confusing things earthly (the Greek philosophy itself) with things heavenly (ultimate truth about God and salvation), but by building from earth to heaven using the natural revelation his hearers had, then jettisoning the ladder once he reached the discussion of those matters reserved for special revelation (Scripture). Natural revelation (in this case, the truth within Greek philosophy) was very helpful as far as it went, but to continue the discussion and actually proclaim the truth about God and the human condition, judgment, and salvation, the apostle had to rely on special revelation: the record of the doing and dying of Christ, His resurrection, and His right to judge. Paul understood and exploited the truth in the secular worldview, but then he judged the errors by Scripture.

Those who do not know the strength of that which is part of the unbeliever's slavery will never know how to free him or her. This does not mean that every Christian must suddenly become an expert on all of the branches of wisdom and knowledge in human history, but it does mean that the Christian witness cannot be naive. It cannot simply ridicule unbelief.

As we have seen, there are great dangers in ignoring the secular mind—not only because, as Calvin said, we miss God's gifts distributed even to unbelievers in His common grace, but because we are left with no way of knowing the extent to which we ourselves are being shaped, albeit indirectly, by these trends in secular thought. By reading James's *Pragmatism* or Mill's treatise on *Utilitarianism,* we begin to recognize some of the forces that have shaped our culture and, therefore, our own thinking as Christians. We cannot be divorced from our time and place any more than an Asian or an African can be, and it is naive to think that we just read the Bible, without any cultural blinders. In order to judge our ideas, we must know two things as well as we possibly can: the forces of the world, shaping our thoughts, and the truths of Scripture, correcting our thoughts and revealing God and His saving promises to us. Those who do not care to read secular books will be impoverished and will be susceptible to subtle and indirect seduction, while those who do not carefully study Scripture will lose their only plumb line for judging truth from error, belief from unbelief, right from wrong. Those who know Scripture *and* their culture have the ability to recognize truth and to reject falsehood when they hear or read it—in secular literature or from the pulpit.

AVOIDING THE TWO DANGERS

The Reformers attacked the "Sophists" who had turned the clear teaching of Scripture into puzzles while they had, meanwhile, turned to secular wisdom to answer the questions for which the Bible seemed to them insufficient. It would be a mistake to see the Reformers as anti-philosophical or anti-intellectual, since they were champions of learning's renaissance. Even Luther's rambunctious references to reason as "the devil's whore" must be understood in the light of the sixteenth-century battle: Human reason, which can never know that God is a forgiving God who sent Christ as the sinner's substitute, must never be given the place of shaping theology. When it is given that place, it always turns the Gospel into some form of works-righteousness, because that is what makes sense to the fallen heart. "The message of the cross is foolishness to those who are perishing," Paul said in 1 Corinthians 1, not because it is illogical or rationally indefensible; not because it requires a leap of stupidity, often called "faith." It is foolishness even to those who are convinced of its arguments. Pinchas Lapide, the eminent modern Jewish scholar who argued for the resurrection as a historical event, nevertheless expressed absolutely no interest in it as a solution to the problem between God and himself. It is foolishness because we do not really believe we are sinners and that God is really holy. The Cross misses us completely.

But what do we make of Tertullian's argument: "After Jesus Christ we have no need of speculation, after the Gospel no need of research. When we come to believe, we have no desire to believe anything else; for we begin by believing that there is nothing else which we have to believe"? This is, of course, where many contemporary Christians find themselves. But it confuses things heavenly and things earthly. Just because secular wisdom and knowledge cannot navigate the way to God through Christ does not mean that it cannot navigate the Atlantic Ocean! Just because we cannot find salvation through the great philosophers does not mean that "we have no desire to believe anything else" that is not dependent on special revelation. That would render reading, writing, and arithmetic quite frivolous indeed. And simply because we cannot learn about the Cross as God's plan of redemption from the arts and sciences does not mean that "after the Gospel [there is] no need of research." Think of the many victims of disease who have profited from the research of diligent scientists, regardless of those researchers' religious commitments. There is much worth knowing about things earthly that the Bible does not take the time to tell us. And yet, there is nothing about God, ourselves, and our relationship to God that the world can tell us more truthfully or wonderfully than God Himself has in His infallible Word.

With this business of "vain philosophy," then, we must beware of the two dangers: The first danger is to ignore the promises and perils of human wisdom. God gave and gives even unbelievers wisdom, justice, and civil righteousness. Even though these gifts are merely tokens of common rather than saving grace, they are not to be taken lightly. There is, therefore, no need to trivialize things earthly by feeling the need to "baptize" everything with religion.

But we must also beware of the effects of secular thought on our own thinking and lifestyle at the point where these forces do clash with Scripture. There is nothing more obnoxious than the fellow who proudly despises "worldly wisdom" and avoids the study of secular disciplines, literature, and film while he displays his indebtedness to secular psychology, marketing, politics, and sociology in his own unsophisticated style. I think of the pastor who warned me against reading secular authors, while he himself speculated on the day of Christ's return by appealing to current events in the newspaper, shared "biblical" tips for self-esteem (a major topic in the Bible, if you're looking for it, it would appear), and discovered the "biblical" position on every conceivable political issue. This pastor was shaped by secular wisdom just as surely as anyone else, but because he refused to see that "trickle-down" effect in his own thinking (since he did not receive it directly from reading the secular authors), he was, ironically, more prone to mistaking it for the Word of God.

Just as the defendant who cannot afford an attorney will nevertheless be given one by the court, so too every person has a philosophical outlook that even influences the way he or she reads the Bible—regardless of whether it comes through reading Sartre or watching Oprah, whether sophisticated and urbane or superficial and of only passing relevance. It is an outlook that is either actively pursued or passively received by osmosis. If we naively assume that we are unaffected by our own context, we will miss the ways in which we are unfaithful to the biblical text because of our hidden prejudices. We must bring those prejudices of time and place into the open, judge them by the Word, and hold on to that which is good. We must appreciate secular wisdom, culture, art, and thought so that we can resist its force with better arguments, both for our own good and the good of others, but we must also appreciate it because, as Calvin warned, scorning it would cast a great aspersion upon the very Holy Spirit who showers even His enemies with gifts of common grace.

We come full circle, then, to our opening story. What are we to do with Elizabeth? Or rather, what is Elizabeth to do with us? Is she to make a choice between being Christ's disciple and a pupil of the philosophers?

As we have seen, no such choice is required of a Christian, so long as secular wisdom—whether philosophy, psychology, sociology, marketing, business principles, etc.—is not allowed priority in explaining "things heavenly." When Nebuchadnezzar, king of Babylon, plundered Jerusalem, he carried off more than the gold from the temple. We read:

> Then the king ordered Ashpenaz, chief of his court officials, to bring in some of the Israelites from the royal family and the nobility—young men without any physical defect, handsome, showing aptitude for every kind of learning, well informed, quick to understand, and qualified to serve in the king's palace. He was

to teach them the language and literature of the Babylonians. The king assigned them a daily amount of food and wine from the king's table. They were to be trained for three years, and after that they were to enter the king's service. (Daniel 1:3–5)

In order to prove their reliance on God rather than a pagan king, Daniel and his fellow Jewish court pupils refused the delightful fare of the king's table. Nevertheless, they learned Babylonian language and literature. Not only was this secular learning acceptable to God; we read the following: "To these four young men *God gave* knowledge and understanding of all kinds of literature and learning. . . . In every matter of wisdom and understanding about which the king questioned them, he found them ten times better than all the magicians and enchanters in his whole kingdom" (Daniel 1:17, 20, italics added).

Imagine that: Even as slaves in Babylon, God's people were not only allowed, but prepared by God, to excel in secular learning. Centuries before, Joseph had risen to a similar prominence in Egypt, winning Pharaoh's admiration for his brilliance and learning. As Egypt's prime minister, second in command only to Pharaoh himself, Joseph gave his full energies to the secular task before him.

Because God has created this world and upholds it by His gracious providence, there is no secular activity that is barred from Christians, unless that activity is specifically forbidden by God in Scripture. It does not have to be "Christianized" or "spiritualized." For instance, we do not need to write *Christian* philosophy or *Christian* music, *Christian* poetry or *Christian* fiction, although we do need Christian theology, worship, evangelism, and ethics. Daniel and Joseph knew how to excel in secular learning while maintaining their deepest convictions drawn from the inexhaustible well of biblical revelation.

That is not to say that those who attempt to build bridges between Christianity and philosophy, the arts, and science are in error, but it is to say that the realm of "common grace" is just that—common. It is not specifically Christian (i.e., redeemed), even though God rules over it and sees to it that culture prospers. Christians should be engaged in these fields, but not in order to "take them back" or redeem them; but rather, to fulfill their divinely ordained callings in the world.

Elizabeth, therefore, need not fear the secular nature of her studies, but she should rely on God's fatherly goodness in giving her the talent and the opportunity for exercising her calling to the glory of God.

NOTES

1. Hugh T. Kerr, ed., *Readings in Christian Thought* (Nashville: Abingdon, 1966), 38–39.
2. John Calvin, *Institutes,* 2. 2. 15.

Chapter Four

∎

CHRISTIANITY
AND
THE ARTS

∎

How many times have you heard Christians admit somewhat apologetically to having just finished reading a secular novel? Do you ever get tired of seeing the same few mediocre Christian paintings over and over? Do you feel guilty when you enjoy a film for its artistry or its acting although you recognize that its message is wrong? Although a respectable percentage of art through the centuries has been created by Christians, in our day Christian interaction with the arts is uneasy. Usually, it is limited to producing or enjoying paintings, fiction, or wall hangings with an obvious Christian message. For modern evangelicals, it may not be the work ethic or the fear of misspent time that drives a utilitarianism which destroys the artistic impulse; for many, it is the pragmatism of evangelism and church-related activity.

Denise came to know the Lord in her mid-thirties. It didn't take long for her church to discover that Denise had much to offer its music ministry: She had been trained in opera in Italy and had a beautifully clear soprano. She was recruited to sing in the choir and help lead praise choruses. With the eagerness and fervency common to new adult believers, she enthusiastically took the chance to use her talents for the Lord. Yet one cannot help but wonder how long a person with musical talent and training can be content singing mediocre music—and how guilty the inevitable doubts would leave her feeling. Must a talented believer choose between Christ (leading praise choruses) and the world (singing opera)?

In previous ages, church music was considered "high art"—not because it was "snooty"—after all, Bach created music for the whole church to sing. But it was good music that was and still is recognized as such outside the church. Other Christian musicians had secular employers (especially the royal court). There was a time when Christian artists could pursue quality work because they were accountable to the court or to the church rather than to the multimillion-dollar industry that is Contemporary Christian Music (CCM).

In many evangelical circles, a young artistic genius would be scorned not because his pursuit of the beautiful took time away from his work so much as that it would take time away from "ministry." If a young artist really wanted to serve God with his talents, surely he could find a Christian ministry that would offer a terrific avenue for his gifts. If he simply wanted to make art for its own sake and explore the nature of beauty, that would often be considered a waste of time at best and a flirtation with worldliness at worst. Evangelicalism is predominantly middle-class; there is nothing wrong with that in itself, but it means that whereas the artistic elites (ever since the Romantic period) are treated as Brahmans by the wealthier and better-educated in society, Christians often tend to view them with suspicious apathy. We regard the question of beauty with a certain degree of awkwardness. We just do not sit around and engage in conversations about the nature of beauty.

Someone might reply that Christians do not give much thought to such things because they are not specifically "Christian" questions. While I would agree that these questions are not peculiar to Christians (the subject falls under the heading of creation and common grace), there is no group on earth that should be more interested in asking and pursuing answers to these questions.

But part of the problem is that many contemporary Christians—especially those most closely tied to popular culture (i.e., we evangelicals)—do not even have much of an appreciation for the beauty of the biblical world. I was reminded of this not long ago when a pastor of a megachurch refused to sing an eighteenth-century hymn because of its "thees" and "thous," which he thought made the hymn obsolete. Everyone understands that "thee" and "thou" mean "you," so he could not have meant that the hymn was thereby rendered entirely unintelligible. Obsolete meant something else. He added, "Besides, 'Let angels prostrate fall'? What's *that* all about?" In other words, he did not know what the word "prostrate" meant. But this is not a difficult or insignificant word. It never occurred to him that learning the definition might have aided him in understanding and expressing a posture of godly reverence. Perhaps "I want to praise you, Lord, much more than I do," repeated several times, would be a suitable translation to many. But it does not approach the meaning of the older phrase. We associate moods, attitudes, and even ideas not only with words, but with styles. Angels lying prostrate before the King of kings, when in the context of surrounding joys of the anthem, simply makes the point that individualistic and superficial ditties cannot approach.

The arrogance that this brother attributed to "elitists" who wanted to impose their "snooty" words and music was actually more appropriately his own. Music that has been a vehicle for generations of common believers to express wonder and gratitude at God's graciousness in Christ is now "obsolete" because it does not conform to the tastes of popular youth culture. This is a thorough-going elitism. I am not a "King James Only" person, but I find a negative iconoclasm in contemporary Christianity. Few of the nineteenth-century Romantic hymns, and even fewer of the twentieth century's "praise and worship" choruses, match the high standards of content and composition that earlier eras maintained. In the Roman Catholic Church the masses of Mozart, Palestrina, Mundy, and Fauré are traded in for guitar-strumming "folk mass," and in Protestantism the great hymns that reflected a God-centered period are traded in for what can only be described as imitations of TV commercials. And there is an arrogance about this, as if those who criticize this "relevant" style for its content or composition suffer from a spiritual malady.

So it will be very difficult for those of us raised to praise banality and ugliness in our own spirituality to appreciate beauty in the secular sphere. If we cannot appreciate the beauty of Elizabethan prose and poetry in the Authorized Version of Scripture, the same suspicions of high (read "difficult") culture will plague us when someone recommends Shakespeare. My own conviction is that it is not the period of music that makes these hymns difficult; in most cases, the music is actually easier to sing. Rather, it is (a) arrogance toward the past and (b) the unfamiliarity of the theology contained in these hymns. Many of us who have been raised in the evangelical world of today, awash in a sea of modernity (marketing, psychology, touchy-feely sentimentalism, individualism, etc.), find ourselves in a foreign land when the focus is on the attributes of God and the truths of redemptive history. In a talk-show culture, it is much easier to talk about ourselves, so "praise songs" reflect this autobiographical (man-centered) focus on me and my experiences, my resolve, my obedience, my happiness and joy, and so on.

As Christopher Lasch pointed out, modern America's characteristic narcissism (self-worship) displays itself through a highly expressive personality. We want to "express ourselves" in praise songs, whereas in the classic hymns before the mid-nineteenth century believers wanted to understand God and redemption, responding both thoughtfully and emotionally. Ironically, this view of worship as "self-expression" (even though we might call it something else) is identical to the secular Romantic idea of art as self-expression. Gone is the view of art as that which expresses the good, the true, and the beautiful. But if we abhor the fact that self-expression as the guiding philosophy of art leads to Maplethorpe's blasphemous pornography, why do we follow the same philosophy in church, if to a much less profane conclusion?

It is true that the Bible does not deal with this question at great length either. But once more we are reminded that we are image-bearing creatures of God Himself, and that we can, therefore, pursue and discern beauty through natural revelation just as the scientist can observe and, to some extent, explain natural phenomena apart from a biblical chapter and verse. In art, we are in the realm of creation again, not redemption; common, not saving grace; the secular, not the sacred. And yet, creation, the common, and the secular all have God's blessing even apart from any usefulness for the church or its evangelistic mission.

In spite of the fact that the Bible is not a textbook in aesthetic theory, there is such a thing as a biblical view of art and its role in society. In working toward a genuinely biblical view, we will use the following questions as our rallying points. In the next chapter we will look further at how individual Christians can better understand and appreciate art.

ARTISTIC CRITERIA

What are the biblical criteria for judging good from bad art?

The simple answer to this question is, "None." In vain does one search the Scriptures for a list of rules for distinguishing good from bad art, literature, or music, rendering any absolutism on the subject somewhat unfounded.

Conservatives must beware of reductionistically compressing this rich variety into a "textbook" view of Scripture.

Here we must be reminded that the artistic sphere is not analyzed in the same way as politics, science, and nonfictional literature. Unlike these disciplines, art is much more than descriptive and didactic, and its purpose is to entertain, to bring pleasure, and to express an idea or perspective on an age that is linked more to the impressions of the imagination than to the arguments and descriptive character of other forms of communication. Unlike the scientist, the artist does not have to account for his or her view of the universe, nor does the description require evidence and experimental observation. Of course, the artist's view of the universe will come through in his work; Stephen Crane and Jean-Paul Sartre hold very different worldviews from George MacDonald, and their fiction reflects that.

For the sake of illustration, let us assume that there are two artists in the same New York studio. Both are commissioned to create works for two very different, yet not unrelated, purposes. One artist is commissioned by the city to create a new and improved road map of New York City and its environs, while the other is selected by a local patron to produce a visionary work capturing the essence of the city. The creator of a road map had better devote painstaking research and detail to his task, but the creator of the visionary painting would expect a great deal of latitude and artistic freedom in her work. The one work would be objective, matter-of-fact, and calculated; the other would be subjective, impressionistic (used here as an adjective, not referring necessarily to the style), and it may not in fact reflect a realistic description from the point of view of the patron. Nevertheless, it will capture a view of the city that eludes a purely descriptive analysis.

Philosopher of science Michael Polanyi has observed, "We know more than we can tell." In other words, through experience, observation, and interaction with nature and other human beings, we have such a wellspring of knowledge that we cannot possibly convert all of the data into language. Even in a rather simple idea (e.g., house, father), there is more than we can express. It is here where the artist is especially equipped to express that which often transcends purely descriptive language. That is why Scripture includes our Lord's parables. A parable is not meant to be taken literally. Of the two commissioned works referred to above (the road map and the painting), the second would correspond to the parable. It is not designed to lay out its truth in propositions, but that does not mean that it is therefore less than truthful, since truth and error are not to be regarded as appearing on a descending scale of proposition and figure of speech (the former being more trustworthy and the latter less so). Jesus' parables are just as true as His propositional statements such as, "I am the Way, the Truth, and the Life." There is a danger in some conservative Christian circles to identify the degree of truth with the degree of literal, propositional form, but Jesus was no less telling the truth when He was using figures of speech.

While modern and postmodern liberals reductionistically compress the rich variety of Scripture—not only the parables, the apocalyptic figures of speech, and poetry, but the historical narratives and propositional statements—to myth and symbol, conservatives must beware of reductionistically compressing this rich variety into a "textbook" view of Scripture. What both liberals and conservatives alike must come to terms with is the Reformation's notion (discovered in Scripture itself) of the grammatico-historical hermeneutic (i.e., method of interpreting a text).

Briefly, this "grammatico-historical" hermeneutic argues that a given biblical text is to be read and interpreted according to the classical rules for interpreting any other literary text. For instance, the story of the Exodus itself (chapters 1–13) is written largely in the genre of a historical narrative, the same genre as a history textbook. There is, therefore, no internal reason (i.e., a reason within the text itself) to read such passages as symbolic or as mythic allegories. But when God declares, "You yourselves have seen what I did to Egypt, and how I carried you on eagles' wings and brought you to myself" (Exodus 19:4), the reader is required to exercise grammatico-historical judgment and recognize that here we have a figure of speech—in this case, a metaphor. In the wake of deconstructionism and the advent of postmodern literary criticism, "metaphor" has come to describe all human language. Everything is a symbol, even fairly straightforward narrative or propositional statements, since words mean whatever the reader or hearer wants them to mean. But in some conservative circles, the opposite reductionism is at work, where even metaphors and similes, allegories and parables, apocalyptic and poetic genres are forced through the grid of literalism. In both of these ways, therefore, the obvious style of a particular text is ignored, in favor of a rather lazy hermeneutic in which everything is either metaphorical or literal. In contrast, the Bible itself is rich with a variety that requires careful distinctions if one is to rightly interpret God's Word. God certainly does not have wings, therefore, nor did He literally carry Israel on eagles' wings. *But that is what the verse said, word for word,* one might object. Yes, but even in straight narrative genres we come across these figures of speech, just as we, in our everyday conversation, will interject common sayings of the time. "It's going to rain cats and dogs" might be interjected into a more sophisticated forecast by a weatherperson on television, but few in the viewing audience would fear a pet invasion as a result of such an expression.

Similarly, when the psalmist declares, "Lord, you have been our dwelling place" (Psalm 90:1), is he intending to suggest that God exists in the shape of a house? And when he says, in the following psalm, "He will cover you with his feathers, and under his wings you will find refuge," is he suggesting that God is a bird? Very few conservatives would take these passages so literally. But isn't that giving up the view that the Bible is the inerrant Word of God and intended to be taken literally, word for word? Not at all. The question here is whether the passage itself requires us to interpret it as other than literal or whether we take a passage that is, by its obvious literary style, meant to be taken literally and declare that it is nonliteral. Both conservatives and liberals must allow the text itself to inform them as to whether a given statement or passage is intended to be taken literally. But even in cases where we come across a figure of speech or a piece of poetry, allegory, parable, or apocalyptic writing, that which is conveyed is literally true, even if the words themselves communicate that truth in a nonliteral manner.

Perhaps another illustration from Scripture will suffice for this point. In Matthew 13, we have a cluster of parables from the lips of Jesus. One of the parables tells the story of the weeds. Like the other parables, this is a fictional story. It is a myth, if you will. In the story, an enemy plants weeds among the wheat in his neighbor's field. The farmer's employees ask him if he wants them to pull up the weeds, but the employer replies that the wheat and the weeds are to be left to grow together until the harvest and then separated.

Jesus did not tell this story as if it ever happened. He did not tell it, for instance, in the same manner in which he states, "For as Jonah was three days and three nights in the belly of a huge fish, so the Son of Man will be three days and three nights in the heart of the earth" (Matthew 12:40). It is a parable, and Jesus told it as such, just as we might sit around the campfire telling stories. The Jewish world was rich with figures of speech and artistic expression, so Jesus explained His mission not only through straightforward propositions, but through other styles, because "we know more than we can tell." Artistic expressions—some poetry, a piece of allegory, a metaphor—often will convey an impression or make a point that actually explains things straightforward propositions simply could not accomplish. And yet, those expressions or figures of speech must not be the basis for building our theology. A corporate executive may actually, over time, find that his or her political views are changing by reading a newspaper's editorials and political cartoons, but when the person turns to the financial page he or she expects direct reporting. "Reading between the lines" is expected in the more artistic expressions, but straight journalistic reporting is expected to be exact in its accuracy. As one would not turn to parables for theology, one would not turn to cartoons for help making decisions regarding the day's business, but truth may be equally conveyed through both. All of Scripture is inerrant, for everything in it is equally inspired by God. But the truth is impressed upon us through a variety of styles and genres.

Later in that chapter in which Jesus told the parable of the wheat and weeds, He explained its meaning. "He answered, 'The one who sowed the good seed is the Son of Man. The field is the world, and the good seed stands for the sons of the kingdom" (Matthew 13:37–38), and on He went to explain this baffling parable. We are all familiar with storytelling, so when Jesus said, "There once was a man . . . ," we read between the lines and realize as the story unfolds that this is probably a parable and not a narrative of an actual historical event. But when His disciples asked Him, "Explain to us the parable of the weeds in the field" (v. 36), that is our signal to look for propositional rather than figurative language. Here we encounter the realm of straightforward statements that may be incorporated into our systematic theology.

This discussion is very important, especially at a time when (a) we tend to associate "literal" with "true" and "symbolic" with "untrue," and (b) we seem to have little interest in good stories, paintings, music, or other forms of artistic expression that do not somehow conform to rationalizations that order (and should order) other forms of communication. Artists do not have any divine edict to be logical, deductive or inductive, realistic or abstract. They are not engaged in *description,* as scientists, mathematicians, historians, and others who must be logical, inductive, and realistic, so they are free to express their own subjective impressions and visions of people, places, ideas, periods, and so forth. Their purpose is not primarily to educate, evangelize, or exhort, but to entertain and to provoke. I say "primarily" because some of the best art and literature does in fact serve a didactic purpose. As a rule, propaganda does not make good art or literature, but sometimes the passion and the rigorous commitment to particular visions and ideas create remarkable exceptions.

"CHRISTIAN ART"

What about "Christian art"? Is there such a thing?

Were great writers and artists of past centuries, like Milton, Bunyan, Handel, and Rembrandt pioneers of "Christian literature and art," or were they simply Christians who created good art? In any secular literature course that still appreciates Western classics, professing Christians dominate the roster, but their works are simply classed as "literary classics." There was no need to create a special class of literature for them, because they have been recognized for their own inherent merit. It is only when our art becomes second-rate that we have to create a special niche for it and justify it by the moral and evangelistic use it serves for the Christian community.

A modern writer who has much to teach us, by instruction and example, in this area is, of course, C. S. Lewis. In one of his letters he wrote, "I do most thoroughly agree with what you say about Art and Literature. To my mind they can only be healthy when they are either (a) admittedly aiming at nothing but innocent recreation or (b) definitely the handmaids of religious or at least moral truth." Those who set out to propagandize through art—whether Marxists or evangelicals—end up trivializing both religion and art. That does not mean that the artist lives unto himself or herself, since artists are responsible to their public. The public does not exist, Lewis reminds us, to serve the artist, but rather the reverse is true. As with any other profession, the artist serves his or her neighbor, but in a manner that is altogether different from other professions.

Lewis observed that "a poetry directly and consciously subordinated to the ends of edification usually becomes bad poetry."[1] There are various factors, of course, that go into producing a work—for instance, a work of fiction. These factors include plot, characterization (development of the people in the piece), setting, and style. These factors alone should guide the artist, but when a specifically *Christian* approach is taken, these factors are often upstaged by moral and evangelistic motives.

Much of Christian music gives the impression that the lyrics and musical composition are incidental to the religious enthusiasm or moral exhortation.

However, that is not to say that there is no place for a distinctively *Christian* or *churchly* art form. Not only should we not dispense with sacred art; we should revive it! Unlike these examples just cited, much of contemporary art, music, and literature apes the world—and the most commercialized version of the world's products. The church wants to be relevant to the whole world, but it must not lose its own distinctiveness in the process. For thousands of years—ever since the temple worship was inaugurated—God's people have struggled to create their own language, a divinely-given frame of reference. It is not only the theological integrity of that language, but the artistic integrity, that Christians have historically considered vital in the service and worship of the Almighty God. Christians should feel free to enjoy and to create popular music, if that is their preference, but is this acceptable in worship? Is the question not at least worth asking when we are talking about the worship of God? After all, worshiping the correct God correctly falls under the judgment of the second commandment. And why must our language in the service descend to the level of the Phil Donahue show? Is the minister's decision to roam casually during a twenty-minute pep talk merely a matter of style, or does it violate God's pattern for the preaching of the Word? The world must not be allowed to tell us how to sing or how to speak in the presence of God. It is God, not the unchurched, who must give us our pattern for worship.

But in this model I am suggesting, it would be perfectly acceptable for a talented Christian singer to find a secular label and record an entire album—even one that never touched on religious themes. Ironically, by suggesting this, Reformation Christians run the risk of being labeled "worldly" by the same individuals who have allowed the world to define their spiritual lives and the art that they produce.

We need better writers, painters, and artists for church liturgy, theology, architecture, and music. We also need better apologists who can interact intelligently with cultural and religious critics of orthodox Christianity. But then we also need better artists on the other side of the line altogether, working side by side daily with unbelievers and experiencing failure and success right along with them. But we will not have these artists, I fear, if we simply collapse all these categories into one lump of mediocrity that takes its cue from the world in the form of mass popular culture.

Much of Christian music gives the impression that the lyrics and musical composition are incidental to the religious enthusiasm or moral exhortation. Thus, the level of actual Christian expression is often as shallow and poorly conceived as the music itself. Contrast modern praise songs with classic hymns from before the nineteenth century and this point will be made plain. Or better yet, contrast "Oh, How He Loves You and Me" or "Shine, Jesus, Shine" with the psalmist's hymn "Have mercy on me, O God, according to your unfailing love; according to your great compassion blot out my transgressions. . . . For I know my transgressions, and my sin is always before me" (Psalm 51:1, 3). It is when we confuse art—poetry, painting, music, fiction, nonfiction—with a means of grace that we, ironically, injure both art and grace. Only the Word and sacraments are God's ordained means of communicating the riches of His favor, so our specifically *Christian* expressions must be framed solely by that rule. This is why the distinction between "secular" and "sacred" ought to be retained. The Reformation did not reject this distinction, but rather the hierarchy attached to it, as if one were more worthwhile or spiritually acceptable to God.

At this point, it might be helpful to see the biblical justification for such a position. When God chose His people and instituted a form of worship, a clear distinction was made between "holy" and "common." As Israel was "holy" and the nations were "common," so God drew a line all the way down to pots and pans. Vessels used in the temple were holy; those used at home were common. Many Christians today, motivated by the best intentions, speak of "the sacredness of all of life." But the ceremonial, civil, and moral laws of God's ancient people clearly distinguished that which was sacred and that which was common. Perhaps what these people are trying to say—and what the Reformation did insist upon—was that God is involved in all of life and is not limited to "religion." That is to say, God is as involved with creation as with redemption, as interested in the common as in the holy. This, of course, is true. In fact, one day, when heaven and earth are once again reunited, the whole world will be redeemed and will once again become the temple of God, His glory filling the earth. Meanwhile, we live in the "in-between" time, when the holy, the church, is separated from the common, the world.

And yet, God's people are still *in* the world, and they live in both the holy and the common spheres of human existence. The medieval church not only distinguished between the holy and the common; it made one "good" and the other "evil," so that the most spiritual Christians were thought to be those who pursued "full-time Christian service" rather than secular (i.e., common) callings. The Reformers, while upholding the biblical distinction between holy and common, insisted that because God created the world and upholds it by His power, it cannot be a realm that is inherently evil. To be sure, it is a battleground in which good and evil, truth and error, belief and unbelief struggle. But so is the church! God upholds both, but they serve two distinct purposes. The purpose of the church is to worship God as He has ordained and to bring the Gospel to the nations. Although the world can be seen by the believer as "a theater of God's glory," as Calvin put it, the world can never be made into a means of redemption. Culture cannot redeem. Art cannot redeem. Science, education, literature, and politics cannot redeem.

This is the knowledge that liberated the great Reformation artists to create works that served both the kingdom of God and the advance of culture in ways that were appropriate to each task, without confusing the two. The church is much richer for the hymns of Charles Wesley, Isaac Watts, Augustus Toplady, and John Newton. They created hymns—a distinct style of music that was neither "highbrow" (the tunes were and still are very easy to master) nor trivial. Far from suggesting that we should have fewer church artists and musicians, I am longing for the recovery of this grand tradition for our own age. But that is not the same as "reaching the unchurched." We do not worship in order to reach the unchurched, but in order to receive God's blessing and to respond in grateful praise. (By evacuating much of the redemptive content from "praise and worship" today, we actually have less that is specifically Christian with which to evangelize the unchurched.) But this does not mean that if one wishes to write books or music for non-Christians that this is unspiritual. It simply means that this is not the purpose for music that is specifically created for divine worship.

If one were to have asked Rembrandt, "Are you a Christian artist?", he would have probably been rather puzzled. Perhaps he might have said, "A Christian, yes, but what do you mean by a 'Christian artist'? Are you suggesting that there is a specific way of artistry that is designated 'Christian'?" And the modern inquirer would probably answer affirmatively. The reason such a question would have been incomprehensible to a Christian artist in such a period is that, at least on the Protestant side, there was a sense of liberation from religiously directed art. While the Counter-Reformation employed thousands of artists in the attempt to recover territory that had been lost to the Reformation, the work that was produced had a religious agenda. It was not, like the so-called Golden Age of literature in Protestant England

and the Golden Age of painting in Protestant Holland, the liberation of artists to simply create good art. It was viewed as a Christian ministry, and Catholic artists were to be grateful that they had been pressed into such a noble service. Much of this art is beautiful and awe-inspiring, but it is obvious in its determination to evoke feelings of otherworldly devotion and piety. The glories of the Roman church are represented in triumphalistic and idealized styles. The same could be said of a good deal of art produced in the Christian world today.

Rembrandt and his contemporaries could move just as easily from a still life or a portrait of the town's cloth guild to a biblical scene, but, as we have seen already in earlier chapters, even these religious subjects were portrayed as real, ordinary people in this world. One notices, in contrast to Counter-Reformation art of the same period, a conspicuous absence of moralism, sentimentalism, and the passion to glorify biblical characters for the purpose of inspiring devotion and imitation.

> *Art and religion require an independent existence—not an unrelated or isolated existence, but a distinct existence.*

In summary, then, the genius of the Reformational approach to the arts is that it makes biblical religion most relevant to artistic endeavor when it is true to itself and frees art to be true to its calling as well. Kuyper observed that, while biblical faith inspires great art, the wedding of religion and art (like the wedding of religion and politics) only ends up destroying both. What do we mean by "Christian" art? Is there a "Christian" style in painting? What is the criterion for determining whether a song is "Christian" rather than secular? Kuyper argued that its *lack* of a special architecture, for instance, makes Reformational Christianity the guardian of good theology and good art, since (unlike Orthodox, Roman Catholic, or Islamic approaches) it refuses to seek to enforce, by propaganda or politics, an artistic form of its religious convictions upon the larger culture. While the Catholic Counter-

Reformation abounded in monuments to the grandeur of Rome, the Reformation itself produced tributes to daily village life and the importance of all human activity, to the glory of God.

This orientation, so obvious in the Dutch Baroque, is also striking in Puritan literature, not least in its sermons. One cannot read these masterpieces of simple exposition without being overwhelmed with the imagery of and allusions to the natural world. While visible images were set before the medieval worshiper, verbal images swept the Puritan saint into the text of Scripture. William Cooper's pleasure in gardens in the presence of urban blandness speaks to this:

> Are they not all proofs
> That man immured in cities, still retains
> His inborn inextinguishable thirst
> Of rural scenes, compensating this loss
> By supplementing shifts, the best he may?

Oxford's Keith Thomas explored this Puritan interest in nature at great length. While the cloistered paradise of the monastery had been the subject of monastic poetry, Puritan poetry, according to Thomas, shifted to the natural world that required no religious justification. "In Post-Reformation literature the enclosed garden was a symbol of repose and harmony," a sort of "outdoor cloister."[2] It is at the highest stage in the development of religion, Kuyper argues, that it does not need the patronage of the arts and vice versa. That does not mean that Christians do not enjoy art, nor that churches themselves are to be ugly, but it does mean that religion must not be reduced to the aesthetic feeling, nor art to the propagation of a particular faith. Kuyper says, however, that religion loses itself in the aesthetic form. "At that period," referring to the "lower form" of the Middle Ages, "all the arts . . . engage in the service of the cult [worship], not merely music, painting, sculpture and architecture, but also the dance, mimicry and the drama."[3] And yet, is this not precisely where evangelicals are today with contemporary "praise and worship"? The Word and sacraments have been pushed into the background, while music, drama, and entertaining productions take center-stage.

This is why art and religion require an independent existence—not an unrelated or isolated existence, but a distinct existence. When Christians lose their faith in the power of the Word, they return to images, but artistic expression is not a reliable path to God any more than the feelings or sentiment of a non-Christian religion. Because biblical faith is based on the announcement of what happened in history, when the God-Man was crucified for our sins and raised for our justification, Christianity is in its greatest danger when sinful creatures (even Christians) attempt to discover religious truth from within. And yet, art is a deeply psychological and emotional enterprise that is meant to satisfy entirely different criteria than that of revealed religion. By definition emanating from the "within-ness" of the artist, art is not supposed to be intellectualized (as Hegel suggested) or spiritualized (as the Romanticists argued and many evangelicals today insist), but accepted for what it is—no more, and no less: a divinely given human activity designed to reflect the truth, beauty, and goodness of the Creator by reflecting on His creation. Even if non-Christians do not recognize this purpose, they cannot help but reflect it, bearing as they do the image of God.

"CHRISTIAN FICTION"

How should we view the attempts of some writers of "Christian fiction"?

The most obvious example of this attempt is the very popular spiritual warfare fiction. The fiction, like much "Christian" fiction, is one-dimensional, lacking in originality and character development. It is obvious that the spiritualized plot is more important than the story itself. Apart from a particular view of the cosmos (light versus darkness, good angels versus bad angels, with Christians determining the outcome), the books could not stand alone as stories.

The Christian public has demanded "Christian" fiction, which is evidently fiction that sanitizes the bad language and lurid scenes, replacing these with wholesome examples and wise exhortation. What readers have actually received, at least by my superficial accounts of the "Christian" fiction that is out there, is neither good theology nor good literature. This is what happens, however, when we confuse creation with redemption: Artistic expression cannot stand alone; it must be justified by a Christian "moral to the story," like Aesop's fables. It must communicate a religious truth and offer moral and spiritual exhortation—that is what makes it uniquely "Christian," but that is also what makes it both bad theology and bad literature. It turns Christianity into moralism rather than a redemptive announcement, and it turns literature into a sermon instead of a story.

In the case of much spiritual warfare fiction, the theology is clearly sub-biblical, since its cosmology (view of the universe) has more in common with the Neoplatonic (gnostic) dualism we have mentioned earlier than with the sovereign God of history who, instead of leaving the outcome of history to sinful creatures (including Christians), "does as he pleases with the powers of heaven and the peoples of the earth" (Daniel 4:35).

One can look at the way in which some Christians have treated C. S. Lewis and his Chronicles of Narnia stories. On more than one occasion I have read or heard criticisms that Lewis's work is "New Age" and borders on the occult. The film version of "The Lion, the Witch, and the Wardrobe," I was once told, leads children into occultic practices. I understand, in a similar vein, that when "Beauty and the Beast" was shown on a Christian college campus, some folks were up in arms because the film, they said, promoted bestiality.

Granted, these are rather extreme examples, but most of us have run across (or perhaps engaged in) this confusion of literary genres. Perhaps we fear that if Christians write myths, especially for children, the children will confuse the myths with biblical stories. But great writers of fiction, like Lewis, knew that there is great power in archetypes. An archetype stands for something else—a prototype in most cases. For instance, Adam, though a real person in history, was an archetype of Christ. In the Chronicles of Narnia, Aslan is archetypical of Christ. Readers may gain a stronger impression of the character of God and His ways with humans by reading this fiction, which never mentions God, the church, or anything else explicitly Christian by name, than in some of his straightforward nonfiction. Like Jesus' parables, fiction does not have to be explicitly Christian. Note how each of our Lord's parables could stand on its own as a story, and they are only seen as explicitly Christian when he explains them in nonfiction terms.

So am I saying that it is acceptable for a Christian to write fiction that is not explicitly Christian, as long as it somehow tries to convey Christian truth through imagery? Actually, although good Christian fiction would conform to C. S. Lewis's example, Christians can go even further without fear of violating their consciences. They may write fairy tales that do not even imply anything specifically Christian or religious. They may create poetry that does not feel a tug toward passing references to God or Christian realities, because all of reality is created and upheld by God whether we mention Him or not—in fact, whether readers believe in Him or not.

Some may assume that I am suggesting that there be no such thing as explicitly Christian art or literature, but that too would be a misunderstanding. Theological writing, religious and moral direction, all have their place as distinct genres, but it is always dangerous to both seriousness and entertainment when they are confused. However, there is an obvious place for explicitly Christian themes in art—whether directed at the general audience or at a specifically Christian audience. Rembrandt's *The Crucifixion* can hang as appropriately in the Chicago Art Institute as in the church narthex: The art is great, even if one does not accept the message that is poignantly conveyed, with the artist including himself as one of those who crucified Christ. Bunyan's *Pilgrim's Progress* is a good piece of fiction in its own right, and that is why it is studied as a Western classic (not in a special category of "Christian literature") in secular classes. The church music of Vivaldi, Bach, and Handel is more famous in many concert halls than in most churches today—not because of the religious themes, but because of the richness of the music. Nor is it illegitimate for a writer to try to persuade readers of his or her point of view, as in Harriet Beecher Stowe's *Uncle Tom's Cabin*. The Jewish writer Chaim Potok writes what might be called "religious fiction," but he presents the world of Judaism "warts and all," leaving the reader with the impression that it is rich and varied, good and bad.

If we are going to write "Christian" literature and create distinctively "Christian" works of art and music, it should be so fully persuasive intellectually and artistically that non-Christians will be impressed with its integrity—even if they disagree. Not long ago, I asked a well-trained musician—a non-Christian—to judge a piece of "praise music." Not knowing my own position, he attempted to express his distaste as tactfully as possible. This stuff is supposed to attract unbelievers, but even in its style (which we consider "relevant") it is shallow and superficial in its imitation of popular music. Another non-Christian friend compares this style to foreign bands that attempt to "make it big" by imitating the American style of pop music. It almost always sounds tacky.

SECULAR AND SACRED

By distinguishing between "secular" and "sacred" art, aren't we right back to the isolationism and separatism that says there is a proper place for Christians over here, but not over there?

Here we do need to be very careful, for a lot of confusion occurs on this very point. It has often been said that the Reformation liberated Christians from viewing the world in terms of a secular/sacred dichotomy. That is true in one sense and false in another. First, it is true that the Reformers denied the Neoplatonic dualism between spirit and matter and insisted that whether one was engaged in ditch-digging or missionary work, rearing children or preaching, all of life was, as Calvin put it, "the marvelous theater of God's glory." No part of human activity was to be seen as somehow outside of God's interest and providential design. Lewis stated that the transformative impulse in Calvin's thought and life "sprang from his refusal to allow the Roman distinction between the life of 'religion' and the life of the world."[4] Nevertheless, the Reformers did distinguish between "things heavenly" and "things earthly," as we have seen. In Scripture, there is an obvious distinction between the holy and the common. Israel was holy, Egypt was common. But that did not mean that Egypt was, therefore, of no concern to God. Even when Joseph ruled Egypt under Pharaoh and Daniel ruled Persia under Nebuchadnezzar, these nations were "common." These nations enjoyed showers upon their crops and God providentially guided them to great discoveries and cultural achievements by natural revelation. But they were not set apart by God as His special people, His redeemed people.

What is true about people is true about things and spheres as well. Since we are not in a national theocracy any longer, cultural activity is not sacred. The Reformation did not deny the distinction between the holy and the common, but it affirmed God's temporal blessing on the latter. It is not that sweeping a floor is somehow a religious or Christian activity, but it glorifies God anyway because it is the image-bearer's service and calling to his or her neighbor.

In his *Julius Caesar,* Handel leads us to wonder and awe of the Creator and Preserver of a world in rebellion; in his *Messiah,* the master leads us to God the Redeemer. These are not two different Gods, but one can honor God in both of His offices.

It is by assuming that there is no distinction between secular and sacred uses that we have almost entirely gutted the great tradition of church music while we have created a style of popular music that is neither truly secular nor truly sacred: Like the fiction, it's bad theology and bad art.

This does not mean, of course, that the Christian songwriter is now free of Christian convictions when he or she sits down at the piano, any more than the Christian politician must set aside his or her biblical beliefs in order to serve the public. It does mean, however, in both cases, that the Christian must participate in culture in a manner that recognizes creation, not redemption, as the appropriate theological basis for such activity. While the Reformers insisted that since we were created in this world, called to this world, and redeemed in this world, we were not to put our faith in the closet when we went to work, they did nevertheless distinguish the church from the world.

Perhaps an illustration will serve to underscore the importance of this matter. Not long ago, I was engaged in a conversation with a number of Christian artists, and one artist commented that too much of contemporary Christian music was simply emotional and lacked biblical content. Another countered, "Yes, but music is by its very nature emotional." These two facts seemed to lead the discussion to an impasse, but this distinction for which I have been arguing came in handy at this point. Both artists were correct. The classic hymns focus on God and His saving work in Christ, since this was the focus of the theology, preaching, teaching, and worship. The nineteenth-century hymns, influenced by Romanticism, focus on my feelings about God and His saving work in Christ. Contemporary "praise music" moves a step further toward the subjective, however, by focusing on my feelings alone, often with very little content relating my feelings to the truth about God and His saving work in Christ. Music—and art in general—should not be forced to always serve a cerebral, intellectual objective that is associated with preaching or reading Scripture or a book of theology. There is nothing wrong with art appealing primarily to the feelings and imagination, but there is a great deal wrong with *worship* that is motivated by feelings and imagination. Therefore, church music should be judged by criteria that are very different from those by which we judge common art. There is nothing unspiritual about enjoying a secular concert simply to be entertained. While we should not be naive about the worldviews that shape secular music or ignore the lyrics because we like the music, we do not have to be rigorously analytical about the music. But we must be rigorously analytical about sacred music. Why? Because it is used not in our own entertainment but in the worship of God! Unfortunately, most of us are more worried about profanity in a Rolling Stones concert than about irreverence in a worship service, but the latter ranks number two in the Ten Commandments. We cannot worship God with our own opinions or emotions; our worship (including the music) must be rigorously checked for its theological integrity. It is not entertainment. That is why I care more about the influence of Carman than the influence of Clapton.

Contemporary Christian music is a new third category. The hymn-writers were church musicians. Some, like Bach and Handel, wrote secular and sacred pieces, but only now do we see an entire style of music that is neither sacred nor secular, but a fusion of both (and again, often a fusion of the worst forms of both). We end up with music that is too religious and otherworldly to get serious airplay on secular stations, but too lacking in transcendence and theological depth to be appropriate for worship. In short, "I Keep Falling in Love with Him Over and Over and Over and Over Again," is, once again, bad theology and bad art. If Christians felt free to write secular love songs (focusing on the horizontal) for secular airplay, and to also write sacred church music of great musical and lyrical depth (focusing on the vertical), perhaps we could see the dawn of a new era of great music in both spheres produced by Christians.

NOTES

1. C. S. Lewis, *Taliessin Through Logres* (Cambridge Univ., 1948), 350–51.
2. Keith Thomas, *Man and the Natural World: A History of the Modern Sensibility* (New York: Pantheon Books, 1983), 235–36.
3. Abraham Kuyper, *Lectures on Calvinism* (Grand Rapids: Eerdmans, 1978), 148.
4. C. S. Lewis, *English Literature in the Sixteenth Century* (London: Oxford Univ., 1973), Introduction, 42.

Chapter Five

■

ART
IN THE
BELIEVER'S
LIFE

■

Owen Warland's artistic genius was incomprehensible to his neighbors and especially to his employer, "old Peter Hovenden." In his story "The Artist of the Beautiful," Nathaniel Hawthorne (1804–64) described the dilemma of a young man whose pursuit of the beautiful was constantly interrupted and set back by the skeptical mortals who failed to see the importance of his spiritual quest. Hovenden, the village watchmaker, had taken Owen under his wing in hopes of tempering the young man's credulity with more practical interests, but he regularly found his young apprentice at work on a delicate piece of art.

After being disturbed in his artistic progress on a number of occasions, Owen gave in to the expectations of the watchmaker, even earning the appreciation of the town for regulating the clock in the church steeple. "The town in general thanked Owen for the punctuality of dinner time." His employer was delighted at the transformation in this young man of promise: "Only get rid altogether of your nonsensical trash about the beautiful, which I nor anybody else, nor yourself to boot, could ever understand,—

only free yourself of that, and your success in life is as sure as daylight," Hovenden admonished. "Thus it is," Hawthorne observed, "that ideas, which grow up within the imagination and appear so lovely to it and of a value beyond whatever men call valuable, are exposed to be shattered and annihilated by contact with the practical."

Owen's slumbering spirit was awakened by the springtime fluttering of the butterflies at the river's edge. He renewed his quest for the beautiful, returning to his delicate project of crafting a butterfly from gold in his shop. He had hoped that at least Annie, old Peter Hovenden's lovely daughter, would understand his mission in life, "for if any human spirit could have sufficiently reverenced the processes so sacred in his eyes, it must have been a woman's."

In sharp contrast to Owen's delicate frame and character was the blacksmith, Robert Danforth. A man of rugged features and large stature, Danforth understood no more than old Peter Hovenden about the spiritual and the beautiful. The townfolk complained that this young man of so much promise "wasted the sunshine . . . in wandering through the woods and fields and along the banks and streams."

Alas, Danforth ended up marrying Annie. When Owen visited the Hovenden house for dinner, he brought a gift. Opening the box, Annie was startled by the fluttering of a butterfly. Not able to discern whether it was mechanical or living, she begged Owen to tell her, but he refused. "Does it matter?" he asked.

The most that the blacksmith could utter was, "Be it what it may, it is a pretty plaything," while old Peter Hovenden merely grinned with incredulity at the whole affair.

Finally, the butterfly lit on the finger of the infant produced by the Danforth union, and the child crushed the beautiful insect in his tiny fist. Annie screamed, while her father laughed scornfully. Robert Danforth pried open his son's fist, "and found within the palm a small heap of glittering fragments, whence the mystery of beauty had fled forever." And yet, for Owen, this was not a tragedy. "He had caught a far other butterfly than this. When the artist rose high enough to achieve the beautiful, the symbol by which he made it perceptible to mortal senses became of little value in his eyes while his spirit possessed itself in the enjoyment of the reality."

Though we must beware of over-intellectualizing a great piece of fiction, throughout the story there is the Romantic antipathy of spirit and matter. The author related the artist's work to the former realm. Owen despises the "practical" and "utilitarian coarseness," but instead strives "to put the very spirit of beauty into form." "Strength is an earthly monster. I make no pretensions to it. My force, whatever there may be of it, is altogether spiritual." The whole question of perpetual motion, related to the timepieces, is only for "men whose brains are mystified with matter, but not me." Danforth's huge physical presence, so utterly material, "darkens and confuses the spiritual element within me." He speaks of "the harsh, material world," and the only way that Annie or anyone else can enter his secret world is by the talisman. The butterfly, "so spirit-like," represents both beauty and the artist, and it alone regarded as "pure, ideal life," whose "airy track would show the path to heaven." The butterfly's material existence was unimportant to Owen now that he had experienced beauty and had "imbibed its spiritual essence." Earlier in the story, Hawthorne made the observation that was finally illustrated in the story's conclusion: "Alas that the artist, whether in poetry, or whatever other material, may not content himself with the inward enjoyment of the beautiful, but must chase the flitting mystery beyond the very realm of his ethereal domain, and crush its frail being in seizing it with a material grasp."

Why do I relate this story from Nathaniel Hawthorne? First of all, it brings together a whole set of questions that need to be raised in talking about art: its purpose, its nature, and its distinct relationship to human activity and culture. We evangelicals regard the question of beauty with a certain degree of awkwardness. We just do not sit around and engage in conversations about the nature of beauty, and we would have great difficulty in understanding Owen's quest. Like the other characters in the story, we would be baffled by the strangeness of his solitude, the intensity of his devotion to a piece of art that served no useful or practical purpose, and the liberation he experienced at the end, with the butterfly crushed, while everyone else stood in horror or scorn.

Hawthorne was part of the Romantic period in literature, corresponding to the Impressionist era in painting. Reacting against the sterility of both Enlightenment rationalism and what they perceived as dry Protestant and Roman Catholic dogmatism, the artists of this age sought to point the way to a more "spiritual" existence. Ralph Waldo Emerson, Walt Whitman, and Henry David Thoreau represent this movement in its extreme, known as Transcendentalism, and these authors championed the idea that the artist (especially the poet) was to be the new priest. (It is no coincidence that Emerson, a Unitarian minister, resigned from the ministry because he thought that the Lord's Supper was too "material" and assumed that a mediator between God and the human spirit was necessary.)

This story of Hawthorne represents the Romantic mood in its revival of Gnosticism. Matter is evil, spirit is good and pure. Physical strength (represented by Danforth), time (represented by Hovenden and the clocks and timepieces that drew Owen away from his real love), matter, and the practical are viewed as antithetical to the physical delicacy (represented both by Owen and Annie), the eternal and the ideal (represented by the butterfly), and the beautiful as an end in itself. The soul, not the body, understands beauty, and a woman (being more emotionally and spiritually sensitive) is therefore more apt to learn the lesson.

Ever since the triumph of this Romantic vision, art has been seen by many as a province for the elite—men and women who have touched the face of God and enjoyed a beatific vision of the elusive trinity of "the true, the good, and the beautiful." Only the artist truly understands the meaning behind reality, while the rest of the world is content to go on leading practical, common, material, and everyday lives. The artist has climbed the ladder into the secret chambers of Paradise and, through his sacramental images, has learned the mysteries that elude the more earthly minded.

As Marxism to an English professor or philosopher, art has become a religion for many ever since the triumph of Romanticism. Thus, as Owen moves from despair to delight that he is the only one "in the know" concerning beauty, so too there is a tendency in modern art to allow artists to get away with this gnostic arrogance. C. S. Lewis wrote of this tendency, "An author should never conceive himself as bringing into existence beauty or wisdom which did not exist before, but simply and solely as trying to embody in terms of his own art some reflection of eternal Beauty and Wisdom." Literature is not the product of spiritual genius and is certainly not self-expression, Lewis insisted, because the artist—regardless of style or medium—is as dependent on reality as the carpenter. While the artist may express his or her own understanding of things, it is after all an understanding *of things* —that is, of persons, places, or things that really do exist and have some recognizable relation to the world observed by common, ordinary people.[1]

> *The sphere of art is distinct from that of the practical and yet is not to be therefore confused with the ultimate.*

As we have already noted concerning the differences between medieval and Reformation painting, so here again we seem to have a view of art in the Romantic period that matches that of the medieval age. First, both periods share an affinity for a Neoplatonic (gnostic) dualism between the realm of spirit (at the top of the ladder) and the realm of matter (at the bottom) and tend to view this world as a mere projection (and a flawed one at that, given its materiality) of heavenly ideas. Therefore, even the earthly subjects in medieval and Romantic painting are not, it seems, portrayed as the final truth, but they always have an ethereal otherworldliness about them. The Annunciation of the Virgin Mary may take place in what is represented as Mary's home, but the home lacks perspective, depth, and common, everyday, earthly objects and surroundings—with the specific purpose of somehow communicating that this is a heavenly encounter. The Reformation artist, however, would represent Mary as a common woman engaged in everyday tasks, with surroundings that would hardly distinguish the painting from an ordinary study in village life during the sixteenth or seventeenth century.

Impressionistic painting, in spite of all of its differences, is nevertheless captured also by this persistent Greek, Neoplatonic vision that captivated the Middle Ages. Hawthorne (and to a greater degree, the Transcendentalists) evidences this perspective in literature.

Nevertheless, Hawthorne's clever story does raise an important issue about the tendency, especially in our modern culture, to judge everything by its practical usefulness. This is the destruction of theology in the churches: "But theology isn't *relevant!*" is what we have heard for years. Similarly, Owen complained that ideas springing from the imagination "are exposed to be shattered and annihilated by contact with the practical," and this is later illustrated by the butterfly losing its color and vigor as long as it lit on the finger of old Peter Hovenden.

Here Abraham Kuyper's insights again are helpful. While he deplored the idolatry of the artistic or aesthetic sphere, Kuyper also warned against the sterile intellectualism that led to Romanticism's reaction:

> Yea, though I admit that the homage of art by the *profanum vulgus* must necessarily lead to art-corruption, nevertheless, in my estimation, even the most injudicious aesthetical fanaticism stands far higher than the common race for wealth, or an unholy prostration before the shrines of Bacchus and Venus. In this cold, irreligious and practical age the warmth of this devotion to art has kept alive many higher aspirations of the soul, which otherwise might readily have died, as they did in the middle of the last [18th] century.[2]

Owen Warland's story also illustrates that the sphere of art is distinct from that of the practical and yet is not to be therefore confused with the ultimate. Art is neither mundane nor redemptive, neither base nor divine. It is a type of worldly endeavor that is unique and justified by considerations belonging to no other discipline or enterprise. The two opposite tendencies are toward materialism and Gnosticism. In Owen Warland's critics we discover the tendency to judge everything, including art, by its usefulness, and in Owen himself we find the tendency to associate art with "the spiritual," as if working with iron were less spiritual simply because of its relation to matter.

Many Christians who are interested in art face the same dilemma that Christians who enjoy philosophy or science deal with: The modern Christian world tends to be suspicious of their spiritual discernment. Like Owen Warland, the Christian artist or art patron risks being misunderstood or standing alone. Yet if beauty is an important part of being human, if appreciating God's creation is a legitimate pursuit for the Christian, and if artistic integrity is more likely to draw the honest pagan than will mediocrity, then these issues are worth looking at. How can a Christian understand art better and help others to appreciate it more? Let's look at a few questions on that subject.

UNDERSTANDING ART

I don't believe that high art (painting, sculpture, classical music, poetry, etc.) is sinful or a distraction, but how can I enjoy it if I don't have any background and training in these fields?

This question is particularly asked in connection with the statement: "I can't understand very much of modern art." The inquirer often concludes that it is his or her own problem and not the artist's. The esoteric elitism of some modern and postmodern art is symptomatic of the shift from art as entertainment and pleasure for the masses to art as a badge of special achievement meant to admit the artist to the balcony, high above public sentiment and taste, to wave graciously and paternalistically to the great unwashed below. Like Owen Warland, they have realized that they are special, unique.

But this was not always so. In fact, art museums are a modern phenomenon. Both Roman Catholic and Protestant art was meant to adorn the space of common people. Regardless of the different views of art's mission and service, both traditions and the artists who represented them believed that their work had to somehow make contact with the public. They did not believe in the self-existent character of their work, as if public tastes were to be entirely disregarded as too crude and base for their self-expression. Art had to be enjoyed, and it was meant to bring delight, wonder, criticism, and even discomfort to the viewer. Just as the Reformation insisted that the common man or woman was to be raised from illiteracy to feast on a common body of literature, so the artist conspired with the writer and musician to create works that could be enjoyed by the masses. Instead of baffling them, it was to elevate them. This was true generally until the Romantic period. Mozart's operas were originally performed for the equivalent of modern moviegoers.

You need not be worried that because you cannot understand much of modern abstract art that you are ill-equipped for the task of enjoying art and literature. (Furthermore, not all of contemporary art is abstract by any means.) Rest assured that if you are reading an author or viewing a painting or hearing a piece of music that was produced prior to the middle of the nineteenth century, the author designed it for your pleasure, not for his or her own esoteric, gnostic self-appreciation. Don't determine your reading list based only on what somebody says you "ought to" like. If you dislike fantasy, Tolkien's lengthy *Lord of the Rings* books will drive you batty. Do you enjoy history, nature stories, mysteries? Start your reading there. Just because there are movies that do not seem to connect with the viewer does not lead to the conclusion that one should abandon all moviegoing, and the same is true of art in general. Note Lewis's remark on this point: "I'm sick of our Abracadabrist poets. What gives the show away is that their professed admirers give quite contradictory interpretations of the same poem—I'm prepared to believe that an unintelligible picture is really a very good horse if all its admirers tell me so; but when one says it's a horse, and the next that it's a ship, and the third that it's an orange, and the fourth that it's Mt. Everest, I give it up."[3]

READING FICTION

Why should we waste our time reading fiction?

One can always pick a fiction-despiser out in a group. Very often, those who do not take the time to read fiction view their world through their own limited perspectives, knowing only their own feelings and thoughts in their own time and place. Just watch one talk show on television for an hour and you will notice that nobody listens, everybody talks. Everyone is preparing the next sentence while the other person (or people, since they are often all speaking at once) addresses the nation. They talk about themselves—their own experiences, habits, opinions, and preferences. In our age of psychobabble, we are turned in on ourselves and our own internal worlds.

To read fiction is to travel to the land of Merlin or the enchanted German forests or to more modern venues, such as Michener's Hawaii, Texas, or South Africa. It is to climb into the rambunctious world of Tolkien's Middle Earth and to read between the lines of Melville's whale and Hawthorne's Salem village. Christians living at the end of the twentieth century are a part of a culture with little historical knowledge or imagination. While we know our own thoughts, imaginations, dreams, and stories, we usually turn to television to "escape" into other worlds, instead of turning to fiction to don the dragon-slayer's coat of armor.

Reading fiction, therefore, not only entertains us (which is reason enough for it); it helps us to step into another time and place and understand a different world and not to simply take our own opinions and experiences as the given truth.

TURNING OFF MTV

How can we get our children interested in reading again, in the age of MTV?

Even before the advent of MTV, C. S. Lewis lamented, "The great authors of the past wrote to entertain the leisure of their adult contemporaries, and a man who cared for literature needed no spur and expected no good conduct marks for sitting down to the food provided for him. Boys at school were taught to read Latin and Greek poetry by the birch, and discovered the English poets as accidentally and naturally as they now discover the local cinema. Most of my own generation, and many, I hope, of yours, tumbled into literature in that fashion."[4] But that last remark is not true of my generation, that of the "Baby boomers," and it is certainly not true of the "Busters."

It is rather remarkable, in fact, that, according to George Barna's surveys, Christian teens watch more MTV than non-Christians. Not only is this dangerous because of the immorally explicit content, but because it undermines one's ability to entertain a single, continuous thought. With its pulsating images, flashing violently and in a disconnected fashion, it trains people to turn their minds off and simply receive. Whereas a piece of fiction requires the reader's involvement at a variety of levels, television in general and MTV in particular reduce the viewer to a passive spectator.

If children are raised with parents reading bedtime stories and are able, as they are growing up, to associate reading with good experiences (the warmth of family and warm fires), they will keep those habits into adulthood. On the other hand, if the TV set was their electronic baby-sitter, whether they were entertained by "Beevis and Butthead" or "McGee and Me," they will not have developed the habit of reading and storytelling. That does not mean that adults who did not grow up reading can never begin, but it does mean that a generation of "channel-surfers" will not be a generation of readers. They will automatically press the button instead of opening the book, because that is how they have learned to spend their leisure.

The good news is that this does not have to be the case, and, happily, many parents are beginning to treat this matter with the seriousness it deserves. Deliberately planning "down" time with their families, they are carving out periods for enjoying Bible reading and catechism, games, books, and even an occasional movie that they can all take pleasure in together. It is just this sort of family routine that will preserve islands of readers, thinkers, and active leaders in a period many are referring to as "the new dark ages," and will, in turn, provide a possible resource for future generations to turn back the night.

THE GOOD, THE TRUE, AND THE BEAUTIFUL

Can it be good if it is not true? Can it be true if it is not beautiful? Can it be beautiful if it is not good?

Many Christians react to the pervasive cultural relativism of our age by insisting that everything—including art—be answerable to an objective set of criteria. Suggesting that there are no such simplistic criteria for art may sound tantamount to saying the same of morality or religion, but this is again to confuse the spheres of human activity.

Aristotle said the greatest good
was happiness, whereas Scripture
declares that it is the glory of God.

Christianity is revealed truth. While some truths about God and the self may be known from nature, the saving message of Christ, the Gospel, is never discovered by human beings. It is always given by God. Not only did God send His Son into the world for salvation, but He also promised the Messiah to the patriarchs and prophets before the Son's incarnation and explained the meaning of those events through His apostles afterward. There is no "Gospel" in nature. That means that however great an unbeliever's knowledge or experience in things "spiritual," he or she is "dead in [his or her] transgressions and sins" (Ephesians 2:1) and incapable of grasping the way of salvation apart from Scripture and the Holy Spirit (1 Corinthians 2:14).

While the Gospel is neither in us by nature (slumbering somewhere in the recesses of our heart, mind, or emotions), nor available to us in nature (for instance, to be discovered by studying the world's religions), much else is. If we want the truth about God's nature, we will not discover the Trinity in physics; if we seek answers to the way of salvation, we will not hear them in a philosophy lecture or be suddenly and intuitively "enlightened" to those answers by viewing a great work of art. But civil morality is not so remote from the heart and mind of fallen humanity, and that is why the apostle, in Romans 1 and 2, emphasizes this sphere as "common ground" between believer and unbeliever.

With this as the background, then, let us reflect on the classical Greek "trinity" of aesthetic virtues: "the good, the true, and the beautiful." Some will recognize an echo in Paul's exhortation: "Finally, brothers, whatever is true, whatever is noble, whatever is right, whatever is pure, whatever is lovely, whatever is admirable—if anything is excellent or praiseworthy—think about such things" (Philippians 4:8). Here, we again come to a point of common ground. Doubtless, Paul was aware of this classical philosophical criterion, and he set his apostolic seal on its truth for God's people. That is not to say that the philosophers correctly understood the ultimate goal of the good (Aristotle said the greatest good was happiness, whereas Scripture declares that it is the glory of God), nor that they were always correct in their identification of that which was good, but there was a great deal of agreement.

In his *Ethics,* Aristotle deemed the chief intellectual virtues to consist of science (demonstrative knowledge of the necessary and eternal), art (knowledge of how to make things), and wisdom: practical wisdom (knowledge of how to secure the ends of human life), intuitive wisdom (knowledge of the principles from which science proceeds), and philosophical wisdom (the union of intuitive reason and science). But we search even the secular philosophers in vain for a list of criteria for judging art.

Even if we take Paul's list: "whatever is true, whatever is noble, whatever is right, whatever is pure, whatever is lovely, whatever is admirable—if anything is excellent or praiseworthy," we still do not have very much to go on as far as a universally binding method of judging good art from bad apart from our own intuitive sense. A group of artists, perhaps all Christians, may be thoroughly convinced that their work conforms to that which is true, noble, right, pure, lovely, admirable, excellent, and praiseworthy, without agreeing on the definitions of those particular characteristics. If that is true of the artists themselves, then it is surely true of their patrons and audience.

For this reason, it is best to be very careful about making absolute judgments about "good" and "bad" art. That is not to say that such judgments cannot be made, for the intuitive sense of the audience is not to be taken lightly. Nevertheless, it is enough to remind us of how often we confuse our tastes and styles with "the good." In art, one man's "good" is another man's "bad," and this artistic relativism often leads modern men and women to conclude that the same is true of religion and morality in general. If we do not distinguish the spheres, we will either create the dogmatism that leads to such relativizing of religion and morality as well, or we will ourselves fall into relativism because we could not tell the difference between the silence of God in providing a criteria for the good in art and in providing such criteria for other spheres of human activity. Because it is more subjective, art is more relative than history, law, philosophy, religion, and ethics.

Our own intuition, therefore, shaped by the scripturally fed and Spirit-illumined conscience, must guide us through this maze of the "good" in art, recalling always that we are in the realm of creation, not redemption; of experience, not revelation.

Does the same go for the true? Is there no way of distinguishing "true" art from "false" art? "True" and "false" may be used in two senses. First, one can mean "true" in relation to the facts. Or, one can mean "true" in terms of judging whether a particular work is worthy of being called art. Let's take it in both senses, beginning with the first.

One can read Sartre's *Nausea* or Camus's *The Rebel,* view a piece of German Expressionism, and listen to a selection from Wagner's *Der Ring des Nibelungen,* and come away with a sense of the artistic expression of an era and a worldview. While these works are all distinct works employing different media, they are windows on the modern, existentialist and nihilistic world. Nevertheless, all of these works are, to my mind, masterpieces. One need not be committed to suicide as the best way out of the human dilemma to appreciate Sartre's despair after two world wars; nor must one be rebellious in order to notice the brutal honesty of Camus and see in his work echoes of Ecclesiastes. German Expressionism, in all of its ugliness, cynicism, and violence, is telling the truth about the human condition in the West in this century, warts and all. And Wagner, Hitler's favorite composer and a devotee of Nietzsche's atheistic nihilism that produced the Holocaust, is now enjoyed by audiences in Tel Aviv.

Often, Christians will boycott authors, movies, or other forms of artistic expression because of the character or religious commitments of the artist, but it is possible to enjoy art without approving of the artist. It is also possible for a particular work to be good in an aesthetic (i.e., artistic) sense, but morally evil, and vice versa. Even in these circumstances, it is not necessarily out of bounds to the Christian (although works that entertain by glorifying depravity can be subtly dangerous). If it were, the description of David's adultery with Bathsheba and murder of Uriah would be unfit for Christian ears, but God is not the prude that we often make Him out to be. In Scripture, we find things that are true but not necessarily good or beautiful.

Where in contemporary Christian music do we find the sentiment expressed by Paul in Romans 7, the experience of a Christian who fails?

Similarly, in Scripture we also find expressions or descriptions that are not true. For instance, there is the stoic theology of Job's friends, who argue at length that if Job is suffering, God must be judging him for some secret sin. Their sermons are recorded at length, and if the book closed with their sermons, we would have no reason for doubting that this was the truth about the problem of evil and suffering. Fortunately God Himself winds the book up with His own series of sermons. Nevertheless, the friends' sermons were part of Scripture, as are the outcries of the psalmist when, at first, he fails to see the truth about God's affairs with human beings. How he envied the wicked, the psalmist confesses: "They have no struggles; their bodies are healthy and strong. . . . Surely in vain have I kept my heart pure; in vain have I washed my hands in innocence" (Psalm 73:4, 13). But his confusion was brought to light when he entered the sanctuary, when he reflected on the eternal, vertical, theological perspective. He realized that the wicked are on slippery ground and that destruction will suddenly come upon them in their prosperity; instead of envying them, now the psalmist flees to the God he has called into question, realizing, "Whom have I in heaven but you? And, being with you, I desire nothing on earth" (v. 25).

It is this rich diversity that we find in Scripture and often so lacking in contemporary Christian expression. We are afraid, it seems, of telling the whole story. Reflecting our American optimism, we shrink at despair, and yet that is a major expression throughout Scripture. James Ward, a Christian musician, has put some of these psalms to music—not just the happy bits, but the depressing sections as well—and he has used the blues style to convey the mood. The style is appropriate to the content.

But in much of contemporary Christian music, the style is on a par with commercial "jingles." In classical church music, we find the choirs moving from one emotion to another depending on the flow of the text. But like the characters in much of "Christian" fiction, a good deal of the "Christian" music today is flat and one-dimensional. It is almost always happy, catchy, and repetitive, not unlike the diet we often get in the evangelical subculture. Where is the terror of God one finds in the prophets? The wrath and judgment, contrasted with the tenderness and justifying mercy of God, that one finds in Jesus Christ? Or where in contemporary Christian music do we find the sentiment expressed by Paul in Romans 7, the experience of a Christian who fails? Is it impossible, given the "victory" emphasis, to express the view of the older hymn-writer, "Prone to wander, Lord, I feel it. Prone to leave the one I love"? By eliminating these features, the Christian experience reflected in the modern genre is out of sync with reality, and the love and tenderness of God in Christ is trivialized into mere sentimentalism. Ironically, such music sets out to conform strictly to Paul's guideline, thinking that this requires the elimination of negative thoughts and expressions that paint a realistic portrait of the human condition, and yet it ends up short on all three counts: It is not good, true, or beautiful.

One can read the poetry of John Donne, a seventeenth-century English preacher and poet, and come across both secular and sacred pieces, but the former glorify God by opening the reader up to the wonders of the creation, while the latter glorify God by direct praise and thanksgiving for His saving work in Christ. There are sonnets in which we find no reference to God or to religious topics, but Donne did not believe that he was therefore secular in his outlook. Donne no more had to justify the goodness of his secular poems by references to God than God Himself had to justify the goodness of His trees, rocks, mountains, valleys, and creatures by stamping His name on everything. Herbert and Milton are other examples of this. John Bunyan wrote *The Pilgrim's Progress* at a time when many Christians were inspired by Reformation theology and the Renaissance allegory. Spenser's *Fairy Queene* was another example of this, and Bunyan was undoubtedly influenced by this marvelous allegory. But even these writers who set out specifically to write Christian allegories recognized that this was not to merely offer a Christian version of popular fiction. It did not advertise itself as general fiction, but, like our Lord's parables, set out to illumine through allegory what others had attempted to explain through doctrinal treatises and sermons. It was both good theology and good allegory because it did not try to do more than it was capable of doing, and the stories could stand on their own as good stories. Centuries of literary critics have insisted upon their categorization as classics of western literature.

Why is it that today so many insist so strongly that Christians can only write, perform, or enjoy "Christian" art and music? And why is so much that is specifically Christian so mediocre? I realize that these judgments are broad-sweeping and that there are Christian artists who are trying to rectify this tendency, but the generalization does seem to be justified given the major currents in contemporary Christian music.

To turn to the world of film, this matter came into sharper focus in a story related to me concerning the movie *Dead Poet's Society,* starring Robin Williams. A woman was watching the film with her younger brother and sister, and all were deeply moved —partly because the family of the boy who commits suicide is similar to their own, but also because it was a good story and portrayed honestly. But this person told me, "If a Christian company had produced the film, it would not have climaxed in existentialist despair—a climax that was true to the film—it would have had the boy discover a tract in the drawer with the gun or otherwise find salvation." She mentioned the film to her brother this past Christmas, only to be "rebuked" because of the movie's unchristian message.

Bad theology leads to bad art, and a theology that only has room for "I can do all things through Christ who strengthens me" and cannot admit "O wretched man that I am. Who will deliver me from this body of death?" will only produce "victory-mode" art that lacks in honesty and truth—two qualities expected especially of Christians and exhibited even on the less pleasant pages of Scripture. Ironically, one may find more that is at least true in a fictional story highlighting an existentialist's despair in the face of life without God than in a Christian's fictional "Star Wars"-like account of cosmic battles decided by creatures rather than the Creator.

One final point deserves to be made. We have been arguing that it is not unacceptable for a Christian to read, watch, or listen to someone or something with which he or she disagrees. Furthermore, even the Bible itself contains good and evil, truth and error (though it does not present evil as good or error as truth); and it does not attempt to cover over the darkness of the human condition, even the condition of believers. But there is a difference between a film such as *Fatal Attraction,* which leaves one appalled at the evil of adultery and a film like *Superman* or *Batman,* in which the hero is seduced and the unwritten assumption is that even superheroes are unfaithful. However, many Christians who would not have allowed their children to see the former had little difficulty sending them off to the latter. *Tombstone* may have had its share of western-style violence, but it was a great story about character, friendship, and loyalty. Steinbeck's novel *East of Eden* is full of moral evil, but the evil is repulsive. But in Hemingway's *For Whom the Bell Tolls,* the main character finds meaning in illicit sex.

From these examples, and many others, we can see that discerning "the true, the good, and the beautiful" can be a complex undertaking. But it is worthwhile, and, more importantly, it is commanded by Scripture (Philippians 4:8).

In our next chapter we will analyze the relationship between Christianity and science. Is there any hope for reconciling this warring couple? We will attempt to discern the common ground and the promises and pitfalls of Christian interaction with that important sphere.

NOTES

1. C. S. Lewis, *Christian Reflections* (Grand Rapids: Eerdmans, 1967), chapters 1, 7.

2. Abraham Kuyper, *Lectures on Calvinism* (Grand Rapids: Eerdmans, 1978), 143.

3. C. S. Lewis, *Selected Literary Essays* (Cambridge Univ.: 1939), 276–77.

4. C. S. Lewis, *Letters to an American Lady* (Grand Rapids: Eerdmans, 1967), 31 March, 1954, 30.

Chapter Six

∎

CHRISTIANITY AND MODERN SCIENCE: CAN'T WE BE FRIENDS?

∎

Abraham Kuyper, Dutch prime minister for the first five years of this century, was also a leader in the arts and sciences. "There is found hidden in Calvinism," he declared in his famous Princeton College addresses, "an impulse, an inclination, an incentive, to scientific investigation. It is a fact that science has been fostered by it, and its principle demands the scientific spirit." And Kuyper supplies ample illustrations of this fact in his own nation's history.[1] The question, "Why was science fostered in Protestant rather than in Roman Catholic lands?" has long occupied the attention of historians. Whatever the many other factors of an economic, social, philosophical, and mechanical nature that doubtless influenced the flowering of modern science, there can be no question that Reformation—that is to say, evangelical Protestant—theology played a decisive role.

But first, let us back up and examine how it was that modern science was born in Christian lands rather than some other context. In a thesis that he has explored in depth in lectures at Oxford, Columbia, and elsewhere, philosopher of science Stanley

L. Jaki has argued that there is a very reasonable explanation for the fact that science as we know it, always stillborn in the great societies of the ancient world and the Muslim empire, nevertheless came to birth and grew to manhood in "Christendom." The belief that Jesus Christ is the only begotten Son of God, Jaki argues, became not only the central affirmation of Christian conviction, but created a cultural nest that was conducive to the "hatching" of this frail and regularly abortive egg. Christian monotheism (faith in one God in three persons) not only explained the scientific facts (order, unity and diversity, etc.), but provided the only rational basis for pursuing those facts.[2]

A similar argument is put forward by one of Britain's most eminent scientists, John Polkinghorne, president of Queen's College, Cambridge, and a former Cambridge University professor of mathematical physics.[3] Polkinghorne insists that theology and science are founded on the same presuppositions about the world: In both faith and science, he says, we must seek to offer explanations of reality—things the way they really are. Instead of blind faith, we should recognize the harmony between natural and special revelation and reject any theory that tells us that we must ignore the facts. This was precisely why science arose in the Christian West in general and especially flowered in Protestant lands: There was a commitment to pursuing the particulars (whether observing the effects of physical laws or examining a biblical doctrine) regardless of the outcome (i.e., even if it contradicted the "universal" or "big picture" perspective that was presupposed by the church). Protestant scientists believed that there were two "books of God"— the book of nature and the book of Scripture—and each provided information that could not be found in the other. Nevertheless, they were not contradictory in their reports. Although Scripture did not address the same questions as science, Scripture was seen as not only consistent with science but, on the most general level, explanatory of the facts that passed under the eyes of scientific investigation.

Another recent philosopher of science who has caused serious rethinking of the intellectual foundations of the scientific enterprise is Thomas Kuhn. In his tour de force, *The Structure of Scientific Revolutions*, Kuhn argued that every major scientific advance is due to a paradigm shift. In the beginning of its rise, science proceeded on the conviction that particular facts would lead one to the universals. Instead of beginning with the conclusion and attempting to secure its support deductively, one should begin with the effects—the smaller pieces of the puzzle—and painstakingly work to fit them where they actually fit instead of attempting to force them into the preconceived spot. But most of these early scientists were Christians and explicitly insisted upon humility in interpreting the ways of God in nature. Even though they employed the inductive method (moving from particulars to universals and from effects to causes rather than vice versa), they knew that they were finite and fallen men and women who required special revelation (Scripture) in order to have the "big picture" to make sense of the whole enterprise.

Intoxicated with its rational and empirical possibilities, the Enlightenment tended to eliminate the need for this special revelation and instead decided that science itself was competent to arrive at the answers to every important question. Where the earlier scientists were able to distinguish between the spheres of science and religion, general and special revelation, common and saving grace, the Enlightenment produced a fundamentally different worldview.

Now, scientists were the new high priests of human knowledge who possessed the key not only to the truth about "things below," but about "things above." Therefore, science has accorded to itself the religious sphere as well. In our time, naturalism, although an unproven presupposition, is the religious commitment that scientific inquiry adopts—much as those earlier scientists presupposed order and rationality on the basis of the universe being God's creation. Ironically, science today often operates on the *philosophical* presupposition that the universe is the product of random chance, yet the entire enterprise has to operate on the *practical* presupposition that there is order and design in order to even justify an eight-hour day in the lab.

Naturalism and chance-theory cannot provide a rational basis for scientific investigation; there can be no stable theories, no physical or natural "laws," no predictability, apart from presupposing order and design. And one cannot presuppose order and design without that leading to some sort of belief about how that order and design came (and comes) to be in a contingent universe. Nevertheless, many scientists (and especially philosophers, who do not actually engage in scientific investigation and, therefore, have the luxury of theorizing in thin air) see their mission not in terms of investigating particulars as expressions of divine order, beauty, and design in the universe, but in terms of explaining the meaning of life. In essence, science not only has jettisoned Scripture as the big-picture explanation of the pieces of the puzzle, but itself seeks now to become revelatory. Stephen Hawking, the well-known Cambridge scientist, is one of many contemporary scientists and philosophers who is convinced that science will eventually crack the combination on the lock of the Heavenly Chamber and steal into the divine mind. Finally, "we shall know the mind of God," Hawking promises.

Without humility, science could never have been born. That is why only those believing scientists, rather than many of the contemporary scientific religionists, could have successfully launched the enterprise. One must constantly revise theories and hypotheses in the light of the facts. Christian humility led many of these earlier scientists to believe not only that they did not know everything, but that it was quite possible, due to both their finitude and the fallenness of the human mind and its powers, to get wrong what they already believed to be true. But secularism has proven just as rigid and dogmatic in its religious presuppositions as the church that refused to hear Galileo because his investigations clashed with their cherished philosophical presuppositions. Not only can science never discover the ultimate meaning of life and things heavenly; it can be wrong about the details of its particular findings and things earthly. Without humility, there can be no genuine scientific advance.

THE RELIGION OF SCIENCE

Like art, science is one of the gods of modernity that our civilization has attempted to enshrine in the place that had been reserved for the triune God. But the facts cannot explain themselves, and we do not interpret them in a vacuum. Our big-picture explanation of the facts may be wrong, and the discovery of any given fact may be allowed to overthrow that universal, ruling picture, but no one can simply string unrelated facts together without attempting some harmony, some larger explanation of the way things are.

Like art, science is increasingly viewed by the layperson with skepticism and cynicism. Instead an enterprise of discovering the marvelous workings of the natural world, science has become for many a religion. Its dogmatic naturalistic foundation is presupposed by the guardians and reigning philosophers. Never mind the facts, we will eventually demonstrate that even though they point to order, design, and a rational Creator, all that we investigate is really the product of random chance and impersonal forces. This is often the unspoken (and sometimes spoken) dogmatism of contemporary philosophers of science, although it is being increasingly undermined by more serious philosophers of science and practicing scientists.

But beyond the thesis that Christianity generally provided the worldview necessary for the rise of modern science, what was it about Protestantism specifically that made it uniquely fertile in this sphere?

Christopher Kaiser is an American theologian who has attempted to interact with this question. There are essentially four theological foundations upon which science flowered, Kaiser maintains: the comprehensibility of the world, the unity of heaven and earth, the relative autonomy of nature, and the ministry of healing and restoration. Kaiser attributes the foundation of science to the effects of the Lutheran and the Calvinistic tradition. In fact, fifty years ago, Robert K. Merton's *Science, Technology and Society in Seventeenth Century England* argued that Puritanism was the most significant single factor in the rise of modern science. Since then, the leading historians of science have agreed.

First, just as we have seen in the realm of the arts, the Reformation created a worldview in which this world took on a new importance. Influenced in part by the Renaissance, the Reformation, nevertheless, took its cue especially from the biblical doctrines of creation, fall, redemption, and restoration. Just as Reformation paintings and literature tended to focus on the wonder, beauty, and simplicity of daily life, so those scientists who were shaped by its thought sought to investigate the technical magnificence of creation for the pursuit of knowledge as well as for the practical benefits such findings would render to their neighbors. But first there had to be a conviction, itself derived from the obvious facts of general observation, that the world was capable of being understood. As Polkinghorne, Jaki, and others argue, modern science could not have been born in a Hindu or Buddhist country, because those religions lack the belief in the comprehensibility of the world. A world of pure enchantment and polytheistic plurality cannot provide a cradle for concepts such as laws of nature, logic, and reason.

As the Reformation liberated laypeople for secular callings . . . so it provided a critical and open spirit for the flowering of the sciences.

This point—the comprehensibility of the world—was also related to the doctrine of secular vocations. Kaiser notes, "In opposition to supporters of papal authority, the Reformers emphasized the divine ordination of Christian laity in secular matters like civil government and the mechanical arts—this was one of the motivations that lay behind their stress on the secular implications of the doctrine of creation."[4] While Rome believed that all truth, whether artistic, scientific, political, philosophical, as well as theological, had been entrusted to her, the Protestants insisted that all authority rested with Scripture, and where Scripture was silent, the church was silent. If the Scriptures did not provide a theory for planetary motion, Christians could entertain opinions, but they had no authority to declare, "Thus sayeth the Lord."

In more extreme forms of medieval mysticism and piety, the gnostic temptation always lurking just beneath the surface of Christendom actually attributed evil to matter and proclaimed a redemption from material existence rather than the redemption *of* material existence. These ideas, even when they were not actually embraced to their full extent, pervaded the medieval mind, but as the Reformation liberated laypeople for secular callings and artistic and philosophical pursuits that were not specifically church-related or gauged by their spiritual or moral applications, so it provided a critical and open spirit for the flowering of the sciences.

Instead of attempting to deduce particulars from universals (for instance, in the case of Galileo and Copernicus, deducing the revolution of the planets from a philosophical commitment that was not biblically required), Protestant scientists were free to study the particulars and arrive at general convictions only after careful examination of the facts led to those conclusions. For this reason, Lewis Spitz, Stanford University historian of the Renaissance and Reformation, argued that Protestantism (and Calvinism in particular) was uniquely suited to produce the empirical epistemology (view of how we know what we know) that gave rise to science.[5]

Bacon, influenced by Calvin and by the Puritans, argued that Aristotelian philosophy had inhibited the progress of science because it told the observer what had to be, regardless of that which was observed. Experiments could not be taken with very great seriousness if we already knew the answer, so the inductive approach (beginning with the little pieces that can be observed and piecing them together into a whole picture) was deemed the only suitable way to get to the bottom of things.

It must be remembered that the founding members of the Royal Society, Britain's leading research fellowship, were Puritans, and their literary interests in the natural world paralleled their scientific pursuits. This is not at all to suggest that only Protestants believed that the world is comprehensible, nor does it mean that Reformation insights alone provided the intellectual foundation for the rise of science. Nevertheless, that worldview undoubtedly contributed factors to the mix that were necessary for the enterprise. For instance, Giordano Bruno, a Dominican priest who converted to Protestantism and studied theology in Geneva, argued in 1584 for a view of the universe's immensity that is just now being demonstrated by science. Bruno was tried and executed for heresy by the Roman Catholic Church, more for his scientific than for his theological views. Kepler became a champion of Copernicus, as were the leading Protestant scientists by this time. As Kaiser points out, Kepler's three laws of planetary orbit laid the foundation for modern astronomy, and the scientist was as grateful to God for these discoveries as he would have been for a discovery of a biblical truth:

> I give you thanks, Creator and God, that you have given me this joy in thy creation, and I rejoice in the works of your hands. See I have now completed the work to which I was called. In it I have used all the talents you have lent to my spirit. I have revealed the majesty of your works to those who will read my words, insofar as my narrow understanding can comprehend their infinite richness.[6]

John Calvin's emphasis on divine providence added another element to this mix. Since God not only created the world, but rules it, there is a certain order in the universe. It is not unwise, therefore, to seek to recognize patterns or laws. To be sure, God was not bound to operate in a particular manner, and He could interrupt these laws or patterns at will (this is where miracles fit), but Calvin observed that in Scripture miracles are always the exception rather than the rule. Science, therefore, could reasonably expect to be able to chronicle a great deal in the way of natural laws and cause and effect without being faced at every turn with the element of chance or unpredictability. Not only was God in charge of salvation and the advance of Christ's kingdom, but He also saw to it that the planets rotated.

THE TWO BOOKS OF GOD

Even the Reformation's central concerns with the doctrine of salvation affected the progress of science, with the former's attention to Scripture as the sole deposit of infallible revelation and with faith alone accepted as the instrument of justification. Whereas Rome had emphasized the perpetuity of revelations and miracles, the Reformation argued that this had led to superstition and undermined biblical authority. A distinction began to emerge especially among Protestants between natural and supernatural spheres, in order to clearly distinguish superstition from the supernatural. The control of the planets and the tides of earth's oceans were just as much the effect of God's work as raising someone from the dead. Yet God carries out one as providence (and it is, therefore, so normal that it may be conformable to certain observable patterns) and the other as miracle (and is, therefore, so extraordinary that it cannot be predicted according to standard, observable laws).

By this doctrine of providence, then, Protestants had a new way of harmonizing these two books of God, natural and special revelation. God was no less at work in the ordinary laws that we call "natural" than in His miraculous activity.

The dangers, of course, of overemphasizing natural laws can be seen in the rise of Deism in the late seventeenth and early eighteenth centuries, flowering into the Enlightenment view of science that has reigned until recently. Eventually, the doctrine of providence was secularized. Instead of being regarded as the activity of God in the *ordinary* execution of His sovereign will, it was increasingly viewed simply as *ordinary*—never mind the "God" part! In other words, it was as if the "laws," which for earlier scientists had merely been human interpretations of the order that God creates and daily upholds, had become gods themselves and, as a watchmaker need only create the watch and wind it up, so God was necessary only to create these laws and set them into motion. The servants became the master: Laws explaining the observable features of God's providence became the *cause* rather than the *effect*. We have here the roots of modern naturalism.

THE SPLIT

You might ask, How did the Reformation resolve the antagonism between faith and science?

Unfortunately, the Reformation did not succeed in this task, but it is important for us to realize that the faith-and-science debate is not only a contemporary phenomenon. Copernicus and Galileo are only the most familiar examples of how dangerous it is to confuse one's philosophical commitments with Scripture, as if to question one is to question the other. Throughout history, we see how easy it is for conservatives to confuse their status quo views with biblical faith, and they may even attach specific proof texts that may at first glance appear to justify those views. Then there is a major discovery and the paradigm shifts. At the time of the Reformation, this happened in the paradigm shift from a Ptolemaic (geocentric) to the Copernican (heliocentric) cosmology (view of the universe). The geocentric, or earth-centered, view insisted that the sun revolves around the earth, while the heliocentric, sun-centered, view countered that the earth revolves around the sun. The Roman church regarded this shift as heretical, but the Reformers questioned it only on scientific and philosophical grounds, and the latter's successors embraced the new worldview.

As we have seen in earlier chapters, the Reformation championed the biblical distinction between the two kingdoms. (This will be especially emphasized in relation to politics.) Luther, Calvin, and the other Reformers believed that although the spheres of church and science were not absolutely autonomous (both depended upon God), science was autonomous from all human authority, including ecclesiastical. As science was freed from the domination of the church, it was increasingly liberated from the restraints of philosophy as well and was able to develop its unique philosophical approach: inductivism based on experimentation and empirical observation.

We have seen how subversive it is to demand that art serve religion, politics, philosophy, or the practical. It is not in the nature of that enterprise to explain reality or to offer accurate propositional accounts; nor is its purpose to order society or lend an artistic justification to a particular ideology. Similarly, science has its own "kingdom" and does not require political, philosophical, religious, or artistic justification. It has its own criteria for its advance.

This raises an important point about the question of what happens when science and Scripture appear to contradict each other. Remembering that God is the author of both, and that imperfect humans can "misread" either, we need humility in determining whether a current scientific model is flawed or whether we are reading into Scripture something that it never intended to say. Bacon imported the "two-kingdoms" approach that had been so influential in the Reformation's view of church and state and applied it to the scientific enterprise. Christ rules in His kingdom through the miracle of grace, but He rules the world through the providence of natural laws. As Kaiser expressed the Baconian ideal, "Nature and grace were two separate kingdoms or depart-ments of the *potentia Dei ordinata* [God's actual reign over the world]: the kingdom of nature was accessible through the arts and sciences based on human reason and observation; the king-dom of God was accessible through the forgiveness of sins based on the teachings of Scripture. Ultimately the two were united in God: one was based on his works; the other on his word."[7] This did not mean that science was not dependent on God's common grace—he emphasized that it was—but it did mean that common grace was not saving grace, and general revelation neither re-quired nor contradicted the facts of special revelation.

Just as some artists have seen their work as in some way sacramental or opening the portals of heaven, many scientists in the Renaissance period saw occultic "sciences" (alchemy, astrol-ogy, etc.) as a secret pathway to spiritual utopia. Political ideolo-gies began to emerge with the same messianic features. Protestants such as Bacon carefully extricated the discipline from such su-perstition. This is especially relevant in our own day, when a growing number of New Age scientists attempt to blend supersti-tion and science.

The most basic method of reasoning
is common sense—even in science.

Finally, Protestantism contributed to the rise of science a view of human culture and activity as *service to neighbor*. In contrast to the esoteric artist or the idealistic politician or the speculative philosopher, the Reformation proposed a view of the common good. The artist is in communion with his or her public, so the work has to in some way connect with them and not sim-ply demonstrate a private spiritual quest. The same was true for all vocations. This idealization of the common good, no doubt, encouraged the steady growth of medicine and other scientific pursuits that not only provided knowledge, but *useful* knowledge for the good of one's neighbor and the larger community. The sixteenth-century English scientist William Turner not only translated the Heidelberg Catechism into English, but he also wrote extensively on the importance of scientists pursuing knowledge for the common good rather than for their own greed and glory. Not only did the Reformed Protestants in England criticize religious superstition, but they also opposed the occultic tendencies that had long been associated with medieval and Renaissance science. In this way they signaled the way for a realistic approach.

COMMON SENSE REALISM

It is beyond the scope of this chapter to analyze the many developments that eventually undermined the harmonic bond between science and faith, but suffice it to say that when science —largely through the influence of Immanuel Kant (1724–1804) —maintained that faith rested on a nonrational and nonempirical foundation, there was no longer an intellectually justifiable unity between the two spheres. As distinct as they were and as different as their sources might be, it was once believed that faith and reason were equally accessible to human inquiry. When pietism began to stress the inwardness of Christian experience over reason and external, objective facts, those who had been influenced by that background, such as Kant, advocated a divorce of the two spheres. Consequently, Kant insisted that faith belonged in the noumenal realm ("the spiritual"), while scientific investigation was concerned with the phenomenal realm (i.e., where things actually happen that may be observed or rationally proven). Kant continued to believe in the existence of God, but only because he had to presuppose His existence in order to have morality, order, and meaning. Believing that faith was now safely removed to a nonrational realm, free from the assaults of intellectual and scientific criticism, Kant actually opened the way to disregarding religion as insignificant and unknowable. Only that which one could observe and examine through scientific observation could be truly "known" as a fact.

Against this view, the Scottish Enlightenment produced some figures who challenged these continental Enlightenment influences. Thomas Reid (1710–96), for instance, argued for "Common Sense Realism" as the most basic way of arriving at truth in any discipline. Through Sir William Hamilton and the Presbyterian theologians who adopted this position, it became the dominant philosophy in American education well into the last century.[8] As we have criticized the "elitist" theories of art, philosophy, and science, so Reid ruthlessly criticized those who would create a method of discovering the truth about things on any basis other than that understood by the common person. That is not because Reid was a populist who wanted to reduce everything to the lowest common denominator, but because he believed that, at the end of the day, the method of reasoning that a philosopher and a milkmaid use to decide matters of daily life (viz., whether it's safe to cross the street when cars are passing) is the same method of reasoning that anyone should employ in order to arrive at truth. Why would one use common sense in daily decisions about reality and then employ some other, ostensibly higher method of attaining certainty for other decisions?

Reid's essential presupposition is that the human faculties of sense and memory are basically reliable. To be sure, they do not produce absolute certainty, but when one is crossing the street, the question of absolute certainty is not all that important. One senses impending danger and, using his or her common sense, avoids oncoming vehicles. One does not stop to invent a syllogistic argument (Cars frequently use streets. This is a street. Therefore, cars frequently use this street), as employed by rationalists. Nor does one conduct an experiment. These may be useful methods at arriving at some conclusions, but the most basic method of reasoning is common sense—even in science.

This assumes that there is such a thing as a real world (which we have seen is a basic assumption of Protestantism that led to the rise of science in the first place) and that that real world is capable of being understood in some degree. What we experience with our senses and memory are not merely our own ideas, which we force onto that reality, but the direct apprehension of reality itself. At first, this might sound like a pedantic subject, but it is utterly foundational to the most basic questions of how we know what we know. Whereas Descartes and Kant insisted that our ideas (presuppositions in the mind) shape our understanding of reality, much the way the cookie cutter shapes cookies or an ice-cube tray shapes ice, Reid followed the realist approach. What we observe shapes what we know and believe and is not simply forced into patterns by the mind. To what extent do our ideas and interpretations, biases and presuppositions, determine what we believe and why we believe it? To what extent *should* they? Is it naive to believe that our perceptions of reality are determined by reality rather than by the mind? Or is that in fact the goal of the knower: to attempt, insofar as it is possible, to understand reality directly, without prejudices or *a priori* commitments? Common Sense Realism opts for the latter interpretation. The evidence outside our own ideas and presuppositions of reason can actually alter and overthrow the latter.

If Kant's rationalism and Hegel's idealism were not enough to strip the knower of his confidence in the objective world and in the knowability of reality, the crisis is much more acute in our day. Rationalism and idealism have insisted that there is no reality independent of the mind. The postmodern condition in which we now find ourselves only accentuates that belief. With the collapse of the modern experiment in reason without God came disillusionment with reason itself. We have now come to believe that there is no such thing as absolute truth. Jacques Derrida led the charge of the literary deconstructionists. Deconstructionists believe that texts, secular or religious, do not even have any objective meaning, but have their meaning assigned to them by the reader rather than by the author.

It is interesting that this same agenda, which began in literature, has achieved credence only among *philosophers* of science rather than practicing scientists. As Polkinghorne remarked, "Yet it is from the sidelines that these sceptical voices are raised. Very few of those actually engaged in scientific work doubt that they are learning about the actual pattern and process of the physical world."[9] With certain modifications, Michael Polanyi, another famous philosopher of science, argued that induction and Common Sense Realism are not only fundamental to science, but to the existence and activity of the average human being. One does not infer what must be true and then find facts to support it, but one begins with a few facts and a working hypothesis, ever ready to revise the hypothesis when the facts require.

EVIDENTIALISM

J. R. Carnes, a mathematician, states that theology "stands in exactly the same relation to religious experience as scientific theory does to our ordinary experience of the world."[10] That, of course, raises an important question: Does that mean that doctrine is formed on the basis of natural theology or human experience instead of upon the Word of God? That question relates to a position in contemporary apologetics known as "evidentialism."

Mediated through the Common Sense Realists in Scotland and America, and integrated into the apologetics of Princeton Theological Seminary during its heyday (late nineteenth century) under B. B. Warfield and the Hodges, "evidentialism" became the apologetic method of a number of evangelicals in this century, most notably John Warwick Montgomery. Like its parent, evidentialism maintains that reality is knowable and that one should make decisions about truth the same way one makes decisions about the smallest details of daily life. In answer to the question of whether theology is to religious experience what science is to experience of the natural world, evidentialism would reply, yes and no: no in the sense that the doctrine of the Trinity, for instance, cannot be discovered from religious experience. If religious experience determined revealed truth, there would be no end to the craziness! Nevertheless, as we have seen, there is a good deal that can be known in nature (and human experience) that we can see and know before we know the truth of Scripture.

Here, evidentialism would begin with the historical fact of the Resurrection and invite the skeptic to treat the matter as one would any piece of history. The historian begins with primary documents to determine the reliability of a historical account, and he or she begins with the most reliable of those primary documents. The most reliable documents are the oldest, because they must be closest to the time of the actual event for an accurate report: Stories inflate over time. Since miracles are extraordinary, there must be a critical skepticism. That is, the reports must not be carelessly accepted. The documents must be analyzed for their authenticity, as any other historical account, and even more scrupulously because of the nature of their claims. The documents must have been written by people who were close enough to the parties and events involved to have a first-hand account. If these reports were widely available to the public, including enemies, there is a very great interest on the part of the historian in finding out how these reports were received. What were the responses of hostile witnesses—those who had the most to lose if the events were true? What were their best counter-explanations? Are they as plausible as the eyewitness reports? Furthermore, do the accounts have the ring of truth? That is, as one reads them, do the eyewitnesses appear to be credible? If they were placed on a witness stand, would their testimony hold up in a court of law?

In fact, John W. Montgomery has argued that the best model for Christian apologetics is the law-court. Simon Greenleaf, founder of Harvard's Law School, set out to disprove Christian claims by subjecting them to the normal tests for trial law, but Greenleaf ended up being convinced by those very claims on the strength of the witnesses' testimony. Encouraged by Greenleaf's approach, Montgomery, himself a lawyer and a professor of law as well as a theologian, has developed a "common sense" approach to testing the Christian claims. When this apologetic is employed, many discover that the evidence, both internal (within the Scriptures) and external (findings of archaeology, secular historical records and references, etc.), leads to a verdict in favor of those claims. This does not for one moment render the work of the Holy Spirit unnecessary, for some will believe that these events are historical facts but, like the Jewish scholar Pinchas Lapide, conclude that those historical facts have no personal bearing on whether one should become a Christian. Just as the demons accept the historical fact of the resurrection, they do not trust in the resurrected Christ as their justification and redemption. Apologetics is not evangelism, but the former is indispensable to the latter.

PREPARED TO GIVE AN ANSWER

What we are in desperate need of again in our day is a recovery of this "Common Sense Realism" that requires skeptics and Christians to argue their cases on the same basis of intellectual inquiry, instead of the common caricature (made too real by Christians themselves) that "secular" truth (viz., the history of the Battle of Waterloo) can be known by commonsense attention to reports and details, whereas "spiritual" truth (viz., the Resurrection) can only be known by a leap of presumption that we have come to call "faith."

As Polanyi stated, "The possibility of error is a necessary element of any belief bearing on reality. . . . To withhold belief on the grounds of such a hazard is to break off all contact with reality."[11] It may be safer that way, as Kant suggested, but if the Christian claims cannot be, hypothetically speaking, proven wrong, then they cannot be proven to be correct, at least according to normal tests for deciphering true events from fantasy.

We can see that the objections to Christian claims, therefore, do not really come from the realm of science so much as from the realm of theology itself. Ironically, as Basil Mitchell observed, "To deny God's existence on the sole ground that if he existed he would constitute an exception to the manner in which we normally provide identifying references is to beg the question against the theist by demanding that theism accommodate itself to an essentially atheistic metaphysic."[12] In other words, whenever a scientist, philosopher, or historian argues that the Resurrection could not have happened because resurrections don't happen, he is using a circular argument. David Hume, the pivotal Enlightenment philosopher who denied the miraculous, at least realized that he was making an *a priori,* presuppositional commitment to the impossibility of the miraculous, but many scientists and thinkers today naively believe that their rejection of the supernatural, theistic worldview is based on facts, although it is only based on dogmatic, blind faith in naturalism. This is as much fideism (blind attachment to a belief without sufficient reason) as that of the believer who says, "You ask me how I know He lives? He lives within my heart."

All that the Christian requires, arguing on the grounds of Common Sense Realism, is that both parties be willing to work inductively, from particular facts to general conclusions. In the evidentialist scheme, the particular facts surround the event of the Resurrection. If it can be demonstrated that Jesus rose from the dead, then both the records that were judged trustworthy for arriving at that conclusion (the New Testament) and the records to which Jesus, the resurrected Man, gave His approval and authority (the Old Testament) are reliable according to normal, commonsense standards of textual and historical criticism.

By contesting Scripture some of its greatest critics have become convinced of its veracity.

Thus, the orthodox Christian should be the last person on earth to praise the collapse of reason or confidence in the scientific method. It is the philosopher, sitting in his speculative tower, who has the time and leisure to spin imaginary worlds and ideas out of thin air, while the scientist, the lawyer, and the historian have to traffic in the real world of facts. If the Resurrection really happened, it is subject to the tests of truth we apply to other events that really happen; if it is immune or protected from those tests, it will forever be in doubt whether it is a true event, and we will be left in our sins (1 Corinthians 15).

Much space has been taken here to argue for this particular apologetic perspective. I realize that I have neither engaged in the politically charged questions of creation science and evolutionary teaching, nor defended the evidentialist apologetic sufficiently because I have failed to interact with the criticisms made by other apologetic schools (presuppositionalism, either of the Van Til or Gordon Clark varieties, or classical apologetics). Nevertheless, the purpose of this chapter was to invite the average layperson, neither a theologian nor a scientist, to consider the common ground between science and faith. If both secularists and Christians would recognize their prejudices and presuppositions (we all have them) and, acknowledging them, would accept the challenge to engage in a frank discussion of the facts in accordance with this realist approach, there could be more fruitful dialogue in the future. If we do not come to this pass, we will continue the strategy that has given people the impression summarized by Polkinghorne:

> There is a popular caricature which sees the scientist as ever open to the correcting power of new discovery and, in consequence, achieving the reward of real knowledge, whilst the religious believer condemns himself to intellectual imprisonment within the limits of an opinion held on a priori grounds, to which he will cling whatever facts to the contrary. The one is the man of reason; the other blocks the road of honest inquiry with a barrier labeled "incontestable revelation."[13]

This is wrongheaded, writes Polkinghorne, for two reasons: First, it fails to realize that science itself is not quite so cut-and-dried as that. Scientists, too, have to filter their observation through the observation of other phenomena, both their own observations and those of others in many times and places, and they form hypotheses that sometimes inhibit their acceptance of the observable facts. Unlike John Locke's radical empiricism, the common sense realist or "evidentialist" does not say that the mind is a "blank slate," void of presuppositions. What he does insist upon is the potential of external facts to *change* those a priori (prior) commitments. But second, Polkinghorne says that this caricature assumes that, for religion, Scripture is "incontestable revelation." The orthodox believer does not have to hold that the Bible is "incontestable revelation," for by contesting Scripture some of its greatest critics have become convinced of its veracity. If a truth can be proven true, it must also be capable of being found false. Therefore the Christian is not being impious to say, with the great defender of orthodoxy in this century, J. Gresham Machen, "If Jesus is dead, He must be treated as dead. This question must be faced: It is not easy to believe; the resurrection can no longer be accepted as a matter of course. Against it are arrayed mighty resources of modern culture. Traditional, secondhand faith is rapidly being swept away. Faith, in this age, must be of sterner stuff. If it is retained by ignoring facts, it may be useful to the individual, but it will never conquer the world."[14]

Men and women of faith . . . must be
willing to be challenged by science itself.

Nevertheless, when one concludes, on the basis of the particulars, that the Christian claims are true, one submits to Scripture's divine authority without becoming its critic. Once we have reason to conclude that this is divine revelation and not the product of human imagination, speculation, or experience, we have no reason not to submit to it as equivalent to God's direct speech. At that point, theology does not derive its direction from natural theology. This is where we must diverge from Polkinghorne and other non-evangelical scientists. There is a place for natural theology and natural revelation, but once we have been led to embrace the Word of God as the Word of God, we must beware of attempting to find by reason and experience what can be found only in Scripture. We may be able to conclude the Bible's trustworthiness by common sense, rational, evidential inquiry, but we cannot learn the truth about the Trinity, the two natures of Christ, the nature of redemption or things to come by observing nature, by rational reflection, or by human experience.

SPIRITUAL RECOVERY

At the top of our agenda, especially in view of the hostility between faith and science in our day, is the recovery of the doctrinal foundations that helped to foster the environment in which science itself thrived. It is not only science that must give up its dogmatism; we too must recover our confidence in providence. Sometimes we embrace a deistic view, assuming that when legs are lengthened or the dead are raised, God is at work, but when it comes to the normal operations of everyday life, God is uninvolved. Therefore, we either become secular in our worldview Monday through Friday, even though we are religious on Sunday, or we demand a constant flow of the miraculous in order to restore our confidence in God's personal involvement in our lives and in this world. The biblical doctrine of providence is our answer to that problem.

We must also recover the Protestant confidence in the comprehensibility of this world. Rather than pursuing superstitious worldviews that focus on cosmic battles between demons and angels, we should regain our love affair with the material world of God's creation—not in the sense of replacing our hope for heaven with a satisfaction with earth, but in the realization that the entire focus of Christianity and its biblical text is on the unfolding of God's purposes right here in this world, in real human history.

Related to that, we must regain an appreciation for the relative autonomy of nature—not in the sense that nature is autonomous from God, but in the sense that we do not confuse natural revelation and special revelation. Scripture must not be used as a science textbook any more than it is used as a textbook for art or politics. The study of nature is divinely approved because the same God who authored the Scriptures authored this first "book" in creation. While men and women of faith ought to challenge the dogmatic presuppositions of naturalism, they also must be willing to be challenged by science itself. History abounds with examples of how easy it is to wed a particular scientific interpretation to the biblical text, just to have science prove that interpretation wrong. Only later do we learn that the Bible itself never really required such a position, but it is too late: An entire generation is left believing that the Bible was once again overthrown by reason. To speak where God has spoken and to remain silent—or to allow natural revelation to speak—where God has not spoken in Scripture is a great art that we must learn again.

NOTES

1. Abraham Kuyper, *Lectures on Calvinism* (Grand Rapids: Eerdmans, 1973), 110.

2. Stanley L. Jaki, *The Savior of Science* (Washington, D.C.: Regnery Gateway, 1988); *The Road of Science and the Ways of God* (1975 and 1976 Gifford Lectures, University of Edinburgh); *The Origin of Science and the Science of its Origin* (Fremantle Lectures, Oxford, 1977); *Cosmos and Creator* (Oxford).

3. John Polkinghorne, *Reason and Reality: The Relationship Between Science and Theology* (London: SPCK, 1991). See also his *One World* (1986), *Science and Creation* (1988), and *Science and Providence* (1989).

4. Christopher Kaiser, *Creation and the History of Science* (Grand Rapids: Eerdmans, 1991), 121.

5. Lewis Spitz, *The Renaissance and Reformation Movements* (Chicago: Rand McNally, 1971), 580–90. Cf. Alister McGrath, *A Life of John Calvin* (Oxford: Basil Blackwell, 1992).

6. Kaiser, *History of Science,* 127.

7. Ibid., 138. See John Calvin, *Commentary on the First Five Books of Moses,* Genesis, trans. John King (Grand Rapids: Eerdmans, 1948), I, 86.

8. Cf. Thomas Reid, *Essays on the Intellectual Powers of Man,* available in a number of editions and compilations, such as Lewis White Beck, ed., *Eighteenth-Century Philosophy* (New York: The Free Press, 1966).

9. Polkinghorne, *Reason and Reality,* 5.

10. Cited in Polkinghorne, *Reason and Reality,* 4.

11. Ibid., 7.

12. Ibid., 16.

13. Ibid., 49.

14. J. Gresham Machen, *God Transcendent* (Edinburgh: Banner of Truth, 1982), 79.

Chapter Seven

◼

WORKING
FOR THE
WEEKEND

◼

E verybody's working for the week-end," according to the "Lov-
erboy" band's popular song from the eighties. Although it is
difficult to find cultural critics who do not lament the loss of the
work ethic in Western society, placing blame and prophesying
the way forward have become an increasingly tricky business.

For a long time, the views of social economist Max Weber,
who died in 1920, explained the prosperity of Europe and America in terms of the Protestant North and the Catholic South.
Northern Europe, predominantly Protestant, was vigorous in the
wake of the Reformation, whereas the Roman Catholic countries
were often backward and resistant to progress. Weber's thesis
was promulgated under the title of his classic, *The Protestant
Ethic and the Spirit of Capitalism*. Whereas medieval Catholi-
cism had sainted the monk who eschewed worldly activity, Protestantism (and especially Calvinism) called the believer into the
world. The rigor that might have attended the monk's devotion
was now channeled into feverish worldly activity. Weber offered
a number of conjectures for why this was so, but they were often

ill-informed theologically. For instance, he suggested that the Calvinist was particularly active in the world in order to prove his election by material prosperity. A cursory glance at the most obvious Reformed and Puritan texts would have forced Weber to rethink this dubious assertion, but it stuck. It is still not uncommon for high school students to find this in their textbooks, even though it has been exploded by historians of every stripe.

While Weber's reading has lost most of its support, the historical consensus continues to affirm that the Protestant Reformation undoubtedly shaped what has even been called the "Protestant" or sometimes "Puritan" work ethic.

Whatever the foundations—we will explore them below—there is no doubt that the biblical doctrines that once supported the Christian's view of work and leisure (and, therefore, shaped the larger culture) are now in eclipse even within conservative circles. As Leland Ryken observes, "Work and leisure are a major concern for both Christians and society at large. We feel guilty about our work, and we feel guilty about our leisure. We do not understand either of them very well."[1]

In the seventies, Charles A. Reich's number one best-seller, *The Greening of America*, predicted a coming revolution due to the disintegration of the Puritan worldview. Although he never hints at being a Christian himself, Reich drew the nation's attention to the remarkable transition from a worldview in which the average individual thought his or her work not only mattered, but contributed to a sense of community and integrity of all of life. Our present society is marked by corruption, crime, and disorder. Individuals feel distanced from the centers of power in an increasingly bureaucratized and centralized society, while the technological revolution and the modern cities that have become its icon leave the individual feeling even less important, less human, and less related to the world around him or her. Further, work and culture seem increasingly artificial, according to Reich. Is there any meaningful work to be done? Are we all to be engaged in making things nobody needs, marketing things that are not only useless, but harmful? "For most Americans, work is mindless, exhausting, boring, servile, and hateful, something to be endured while 'life' is confined to 'time off.'"[2] Further, "America is one vast, terrifying anti-community," since "modern life has obliterated place, locality, and neighborhood, and given us the anonymous separateness of our existence. The family, the most basic social system, has been ruthlessly stripped to its functional essentials. Friendship has been coated over with a layer of impenetrable artificiality as men strive to live roles designed for them."[3] As if all this were not enough, there is a loss of a sense of self. Gone is one's sense of his "imagination, his creativity, his heritage, his dreams, and his personal uniqueness, in order to style him into a productive unit for a mass, technological society."[4]

Granted that Reich was writing on the heels of existential despair during Vietnam, his rather bleak description of modern life is now also being recognized by a small but growing chorus of Christian writers and thinkers.[5] During America's early Puritan phase, there was a social consciousness that tied individuals together, keeping the self from either the meaninglessness of individualism or the meaninglessness of collectivism. But eventually, this foundation eroded and "Each newly sovereign individual could be the source of his own achievement and fulfillment. One worked for oneself, not for society."[6]

We see this even in the average Christian bookstore, where most of the popular books fall into the category of "self-help." Instead of resisting these trends in modernity, Christians have all too often merely lent spiritual respectability to these hedonistic ideas. In this worldview, work loses its significance because man loses his significance before the face of God, and with that loss he also loses his divinely ordained relatedness to others.

How can a modern person make sense of the psalmist's loss in the grandeur of his place in the universe? "When I consider your heavens, the work of your fingers, the moon and the stars, which you have set in place, what is man that you are mindful of him, the son of man that you care for him?" At first, the psalmist's awareness of the vastness of the universe creates a sense of his own smallness, but there is an ironic twist to this contemplation, as he answers his own question: "You made him a little lower than the heavenly beings and crowned him with glory and honor. You made him ruler over the works of your hands; you put everything under his feet. . . . O Lord, our Lord, how majestic is your name in all the earth!" (Psalm 8:5–6, 9). No wonder John Calvin opened his *Institutes* by stating that whether one began with contemplating one's own existence or God's existence, it led to the same place eventually. We do not have an independent existence, but if we jettison God from our worldview (and Christians can do that, too, you know) or push Him into the "spiritual" arena, while our nine-to-five is basically "secular," to that extent the majority of our time will be spent in what we feel to be meaningless activity. It is theology that gives meaning to every activity of human existence.

Because we rarely relate theology to life these days (which is to relate the vertical to the horizontal), we rarely are confronted with the psalmist's reflections. We are rarely captivated with a sense of smallness that turns into a sense of significance based on the calling that God has given to us as His special creatures. The psalmist does not say, after recognizing his relative insignificance in the face of the cosmic scale, "But after all, I am a C.E.O. and have accomplished a lot in my career." Nor does he say, "I may not have climbed the world's corporate ladder, but I've poured my energies into church work." His significance came from the realization not of what he had accomplished, but from the realization that God had assigned a calling to him.

The brilliant Jewish sociologist at Harvard for many years, Daniel Bell, announced rather recently, "We are coming to a watershed in western history" as the social fabric becomes increasingly fragile and disintegrates into a thousand pieces. Inundated with information, we are increasingly ignorant; loaded down with data, we are losing our grip on any wisdom we might have had and are descending into silliness and superstition. And what used to hold everything together? Bell insisted that it was the Protestant worldview, a theological system that was coherent and broad enough to provide a sense of meaning and purpose as much for the day-laborer as for the minister or missionary. Without a sense of the sacred (i.e., transcendence—the feeling that the study of God's greatness inspires, as the psalmist experienced), Bell said there can be no way of making sense of life, including work. At one time, Bell writes, capitalism was rooted in "the Protestant sanctification of work," but secularism has replaced honesty, industry, and neighborly concern with hedonism and self-esteem. "What then can hold the society together?" he asks. Now, we are not responsible citizens, but entitled rights-holders. Work is not a calling, but a job, and it is not *my* duty to serve my neighbor, but someone else's duty (usually the state's).

These, of course, are vast generalizations, but they make sense to most of us in our present situation, because, generalizations or not, there is enough truth to make the point. While the churches pretend that their accommodation to modern hedonism is a "revival," because Americans seem to be eating it up, Bell insisted that it is simply a revival of the spirit of modernity. "If religion is declining," he wrote, "it is because the worldly realm of the sacred has been shrinking. . . . To say that 'God is dead' is, in effect, to say that the social bonds have snapped and that society is dead. . . . To understand the transcendent, man requires a sense of the sacred."[7]

But churches, obsessed with worldly influence and "relevance," have bartered away the only real hope of genuine relevance in the age of spiritual mediocrity and idolatry. When Protestantism was driven by theology (the knowledge, study, contemplation, love, and worship of God in Christ), it provided a genuinely relevant sense of purpose and direction for worldly activity. In other words, once the vertical dimension was clearly corrected and emphasized, the horizontal dimension took its proper shape.

THE PROBLEM OF PIETISM

As we have noted, pietism tended to create a "Christian ghetto" that the Reformation had attempted to dismantle. Called out of the church into the world, evangelicals were again encouraged, especially through the revivalism of the last century-and-a-half, to help build a Christian empire within America. Eventually, we came to the place where we had our own networks, movies, talk shows, cruises, rock stars, entertainers, and other trappings of modern hedonism, without having to bother leaving the ghetto. We called it evangelism, and perhaps we even intended it to be evangelism, but it has ended up only creating a church that is *of* the world but not *in* it, instead of being *in* the world but not *of* it.

> *The individual Christian is in a better place*
> *to witness of his or her faith when that is not*
> *the person's ulterior motive for work.*

Therefore, we often judge our spiritual health in terms of how many people are involved with small groups, Bible studies, prayer circles, and accountability groups; and we are led by the statistics to conclude that we are actually quite vigorous. But Reformation Christianity (i.e., biblical Christianity) should lead us to different standards for judging health: Is the church truly being the church? That is to ask, Is the Word rightly preached? Are the sacraments rightly administered? And is there a healthy concern for and practice of church discipline and good order? If those questions cannot be answered with any degree of confidence, there is no health, regardless of the bustling activity in the ghetto. While the medieval and, to a large extent, pietistic tendency is to call the believer out of the world and into church-related activities, the Reformation approach is to view all church-related activities as "refueling" stations for their real service in the world. We should not put people who work diligently at their calling on a guilt trip for failing to attend every church-related activity or volunteering for church-related tasks. It is the church that serves the Christian so that the Christian can serve God in the world. That is not to say that going to church and participating in a Bible study are merely means to the end of a worldly vocation, since the Word is an end in itself, and we receive God's promises as well as His commands regardless of how useful and practical this may be considered for daily life. But even if a church is feeding the sheep with God's promises, a further question must be asked: If the church itself is healthy internally, are individual Christians fulfilling their calling in the world with excellence? That is not the same question as, Are they winning souls? Rather, Do individual believers sense that it is their *Christian* duty to transcend mediocrity in their daily routines and link their service in the world to their service of an all-knowing God of glory? A Christian does not go to work on Monday morning in order to convert people to Christ, but to pursue his or her calling, for which he or she was designed by divine creation.

This has to be said, not because evangelism is unimportant, but because it is too often assumed by Christians today that work is unimportant, as if its tedious meaninglessness is somehow justified by the opportunities to witness. Some even conclude from this logic that it would be better to abandon the world altogether for the safety of the evangelical ghetto, where one can be assured that his or her work will have a direct evangelistic or church-related objective.

Just as the church, ironically, is most relevant when it is less self-conscious about its relevance and devotes itself to the apostles' teaching, prayer, the sacraments, and fellowship (Acts 2:42), so too the individual Christian is in a better place to witness of his or her faith when that is not the person's ulterior motive for work. When these two factors (the church's faithfulness to its task and the individual believer's faithfulness to his or her calling) converge, we are likely to have more Christians who know their faith well enough to communicate it in casual conversation (without unloading on co-workers with prepackaged scripts), and their excellence at their callings will lend credibility to that profession.

This was precisely the approach to which Paul directed the beleaguered saints in Thessalonica: "Make it your ambition to lead a quiet life, to mind your own business and to work with your hands, just as we told you, so that your daily life may win the respect of outsiders and so that you will not be dependent on anybody" (1 Thessalonians 4:11–12). Some years ago, as *The Christian Yellowpages*, a regional directory of businesses and services that displayed an ichthus (fish) on their logo, arrived in the church narthex, I overheard one businessman tell another: "I'd better snap up one of those so I can figure out who *not* to do business with." Of course, it was sarcastic and uncharitable, but there is a general impression in the minds of both Christians and non-Christians who employ people or engage various services that too often the most zealous Christians end up being the least concerned about their work. Not long ago, a parishioner told me, "I'm liberated from the guilt I used to have for not 'being a witness' at work. I would read my Bible—or, at least, pretend to read it, and pray, and prominently display bumper stickers or posters at my work station. And the more 'guff' I got for being a religious nut, the more spiritual I felt. Now I've taken down the shrine and focus on my work as a reasonable service of worship to God and dedication to my calling, and guess what? Now I'm actually asked about my faith by my co-workers at lunchtime!"

At least in theory, if one has this vertical perspective and views his or her work as service to God and one's neighbor, even the most mundane task can take on significance. John Milton put it in these terms:

> All is, if I have grace to use it so,
> As ever in my great task-master's eye.

In other words, if God gives us the grace to see all of life from His perspective, everything that we do—however menial, however common—is done under the auspices of our divine keeper. George Herbert wrote along a similar vein of sweeping the floor to the glory of God making "that and th'action fine . . . and makes drudgery divine." Is not "drudgery" precisely what contemporary critics are calling the modern experience with regard to work? And is that not too often the experience even of believers?

None of this is to say that work is never drudgery, for that is involved in the curse (Genesis 3). Nor is it to suggest that a believer will never experience job dissatisfaction, or that if he or she does, it is necessarily a sign of God's will to change occupations. Just as sin can smother the joy of our salvation, it can smother the joy of our calling. And it does not even have to be our sin that causes such disappointment. Perhaps it is a harsh employer or distracted employees, or perhaps the "bottom line" keeps one awake into the night. Nevertheless, it does provide some sense of relief and purpose over the long haul to know that it is not my own whimsical and fickle dreams, but ultimately a divine calling, that keeps me at my post in the worst as well as the best of times.

Calvin used this kind of reasoning in defending one's calling:

> Each will bear and swallow the discomforts, vexations, weariness and anxieties in his way of life when he has been persuaded that the burden was laid upon him by God. From this will arise also an impressive consolation: that no task will be so sordid and base, provided you obey your calling in it, that it will not shine and be reckoned very precious in God's sight.

For that reason, "The Lord bids each one of us in all life's actions to look to his calling."[8]

THE BIBLICAL BASIS FOR ONE'S CALLING

We have seen both the problem and the way in which evangelical theology, at its best, addressed the subject of vocation. But what is the biblical foundation for this notion?

The story begins where all stories begin, in the book of Genesis. After the creation of the natural world, something was missing. That is not to say that the Creator forgot something, for this pièce de résistance was placed at the end of the process for good reason. Lush vegetation; abundant creatures of sea, land, and air; restless seas and disruptive skies gave way to tranquillity and order, as God formed the creature who would be His governor of the visible world. "Then God said, 'Let us make man in our image, in our likeness, and let them rule over the fish of the sea and the birds of the air, over the livestock, over all the earth, and over all the creatures that move along the ground.' So God created man in his own image, in the image of God he created him; male and female he created them" (Genesis 1:26–27).

God's delegation of authority was not simply the result of His decree, as if any other animal could have handled the job as efficiently if so selected, but He gave this authority to man because only this creature was singled out to bear His image. Included in this image was a *sensus divinitatus*—a sense of the divine or "transcendence." For this reason, man is *homo reli-*

gionis—intrinsically religious. Even after the Fall, the constant urge to set up idols was an evidence of this intrinsic religious dimension: Man cannot live without gods, a sense of the transcendent. Every human activity was designed to be inherently religious, from the planting of crops (agriculture) to the naming of animals (zoology).

Man was created, both male and female, to reflect God's image at least in part by exercising one's vocation or calling in the world. The world was to be governed, but not exploited, by man, and man would give an account to God Himself for the rule exercised over creation.

> *The restoration's certainty (because of Christ's resurrection) gives us hope for our daily tasks in the world.*

But, as we know, man refused to *reflect* divine glory; he wanted to be God himself—not a creature, but an autonomous creator.

We must be careful not to view the Fall in exclusively individualistic terms. Sometimes, we are so understandably taken with the consequences of the Fall for personal alienation from God that we ignore the vast cosmic effects that are recorded in Genesis. The curse for Adam's transgression fell not only on the human-divine relationship, but on the ground, on childbirth, on daily life in the world. No longer was this world one great cathedral of the divine blessing, but it had become a battleground for the civil war between the builders of God's city and those whose faith is in the cities of this world.

In spite of that battleground, we are heartened by God's grace. Not only did God promise a Messiah to Adam and Eve and to all who would trust in His promise; He promised the restoration of the entire created order that, through no fault of its own, was plunged with its divine-image-bearing underlord into disorder and rebellion. Although we are still awaiting this restoration, it is as much the believer's hope as his or her own resurrection from the dead (Romans 8:22–25). This keeps us from either apathy or triumphalism, since the restoration's certainty (because of Christ's resurrection) gives us hope for our daily tasks in the world, but its fulfillment in the future forces us to patiently await its consummation.

But we are not only heartened by God's saving grace, which includes the creation as well as individuals. That would be little comfort to us if we had to think of this present age as nothing more than a battlefield between saints and the damned. God adds to the comfort of saving grace the blessing of common grace. As we have already seen, common grace is God's *temporal* restraint of both human wickedness and His own wrath that must eventually set things straight. In this present evil age, "He causes his sun to rise on the evil and the good, and sends rain on the righteous and the unrighteous," and requires us to have the same mind (Matthew 5:45).

This means that if God, being righteous, can endure the evil of our own hearts as His children, much less the rebellion of unbelievers, then surely we, being unrighteous, must bear the unbelief and wickedness of our neighbors and co-workers. This does not mean that we never raise our voices against unbelief and vice, but it does mean that God's common grace is sufficient for building a common civilization and working together side by side with those who do not share our beliefs, convictions, attitudes, or worldview.

Now, in other words, work is no longer a sacred activity, but it is still a creation ordinance. That is, this secular calling is a divine gift given to believer and unbeliever alike. Christians are not unique in their giftedness for a particular vocation, but they are uniquely responsible to exercise that calling with diligence and faithfulness. Employees are commanded to obey their employers "with respect and fear, and with sincerity of heart, just as you would obey Christ" (Ephesians 6:5). Paul declares, "Obey them not only to win their favor when their eye is on you, but like slaves of Christ, doing the will of God from your heart. Serve wholeheartedly, as if you were serving the Lord, not men, because you know that the Lord will reward everyone for whatever good he does, whether he is slave or free" (vv. 6–8). But employers are equally bound by their calling to treat their employees "in the same way," a somewhat radical view in Paul's day. "Do not threaten them, since you know that he who is both their Master and yours is in heaven, and there is no favoritism with him" (v. 9). The world may say that the boss has unlimited authority and power, but God Himself is the "boss" of earth's "bosses," and He does not judge according to earthly rank.

In summary, then, the biblical concept of work is very different from the perception one finds all too common in Christian circles. Too often one discerns an attitude toward work that suggests that people consider work a necessary evil, a consequence of the Fall, like government. While that is true of government, it is not true of work any more than it is true of the family or the church. Work is a divine institution of *Creation,* given to man as a sign of his dignity, not a curse of the Fall. It is now given to the believer to recover the transcendent dimension and connect his or her daily life in this world to the life in heaven, where we are seated with Christ in heavenly places, and to the life to come, where we will reign with Christ in Paradise Restored.

WHAT ABOUT WEEKENDS?

Some Christians (like non-Christians) suffer from apathy, but others suffer from "workaholism"—an addiction to stress and worldly activity. Just as surely as the biblical view calls us to diligent worldly activity, it calls us to take rest seriously. This is not merely a health concern, although that is part of it, since God is as concerned with our bodies as with our souls. But just as God created man to imitate His "worldliness" (i.e., work in creation), His image is a summons to imitate His rest. This is what we find in the very order of God's creation: There are six days of work and a seventh day of rest.

Throughout the Old Testament, this pattern of work and rest is repeated. God encoded this into the very fabric of His theocracy (Exodus 20:8–10; 31:14; Leviticus 25:2; Deuteronomy 5:12–15; Isaiah 56:2–7), so that the people understood that they were entering into God's promised rest.

Although this principle of rest was written into the fabric of the human body and soul at Creation, it took on a very different

148

primary purpose after the Fall. True rest was spiritual rest, for even a tired body can be refreshed with the confidence that God is merciful, but the most vigorous frame is weary if the soul is restless and desperate. After the Fall, God invited His people to enter His eternal rest, the "seventh day" that has been and will forever continue to be God's very own "place" and "time"—an infinitude of rest and delight in God.

When God so strictly framed the Sabbaths then, the intention was to point forward to the "narrow way" of salvation in Christ. Many seek to work not only for their daily bread, but for their eternal forgiveness as well, and this is precisely what Jesus was talking about when He discussed the "Sabbath rest" in Matthew 12. Very often, Matthew's gospel will record an announcement from Jesus concerning His mission and then relate a narrative account of Jesus' ministry that somehow made sense of the announcement. This is the case when Jesus warmly invites, "Come to me, all you who are weary and burdened, and I will give you rest" (Matthew 11:28). This is an invitation into the "seventh day," sharing God's rest. Right after this announcement, Matthew related the confrontation between the Pharisees and Jesus and His disciples, the latter picking some heads of grain because of their hunger, even though it was the Sabbath. The Pharisees had taken a signpost that had been intended to point the way forward to Christ and an eternal rest from works-righteousness and had turned it into a way of salvation. Ironically, in other words, a shadow pointing to the reality of a free salvation-rest had been turned into the reality itself pointing to a works-salvation. The very thing the Pharisees were determined to forbid on the Sabbath—any kind of human activity—was turned into a form of human activity leading to salvation.

But Jesus declared in that passage that He was the Lord of the Sabbath, and He demonstrated this by healing a man with a shriveled hand before the Pharisees' own eyes on this holy day.

With the resurrection of Christ, the Sabbath has arrived. All who look to Christ for salvation enter it and find rest.

The writer to the Hebrews uses this argument as well, writing to Jewish Christians who were tempted by the persecutions to convert back to Judaism. "Therefore, since the promise of entering his rest still stands, let us be careful that none of you be found to have fallen short of it" (Hebrews 4:1). Notice first of all that if the land of Israel, a geographical plot of ground, had really been the "promised land" in that ultimate sense, and therefore the location of the future kingdom of God, as many today suppose, this biblical writer would not have said that "the promise of entering his rest still stands," since the Jews had been in Palestine for millennia. This same writer makes just that point later in the epistle: The patriarchs "were still living by faith when they died. They did not receive the things promised; they only saw them and welcomed them from a distance" (Hebrews 11:13), looking "for a country of their own" (v. 14). But was this country ultimately the present state of Israel? "Instead, they were longing for a better country—a heavenly one. Therefore God is not ashamed to be called their God, for he has prepared a city for them" (v. 16). Just as He has prepared a holy time (eternal Sabbath), so He has prepared a holy place (heavenly Jeru'salem, which means, "City of Sabbath Rest").

But now back to Hebrews 4, inviting people into the Sabbath rest: "For we also have had the gospel preached to us, just as they [in the Old Testament] did; but the message they heard was of no value to them, because those who heard did not combine it with faith. Now we who have believed enter that rest . . ." (vv. 2–3). The writer raises the matter of the generation that failed to enter the Promised Land because of unbelief, recorded in Numbers 14:21–35. In His anger, God swore that the unbelieving generation "shall never enter my rest," and this is meant to point us to the danger of unbelief. No one has title to the promise apart from faith in Christ. But what does it mean to enter God's rest? Clearly it is more than the earthly Sabbaths that set up holy times for the Jewish calendar. And it is surely more than the physical rest in the land of Canaan, when Israel was led to possess the land under Joshua: "For somewhere he has spoken about the seventh day in these words: 'And on the seventh day God rested from all his work.' . . . For if Joshua had given them rest, God would not have spoken later about another day. There remains, then, a Sabbath-rest for the people of God; for anyone who enters God's rest also rests from his own work, just as God did from his" (Hebrews 4:4, 8–10). That is why the writer follows with a description of "Jesus the Great High Priest," for it is only by His work that we are able to rest—and not only by His work on earth, in His obedient life, death, and glorious resurrection, but in His ascension and in His present intercession on our behalf night and day before the judgment bar of the Divine Majesty. He works so that we may rest.

What does all of this mean for our doctrine of leisure? It seems a bit off-field, but in reality it is the most relevant way of understanding the whole point of leisure. God not only has given us a reason for rest in Creation, which offers temporal rest and pleasure to Christian and non-Christian alike (linked to creation and common grace, not to redemption and saving grace); He has also given to His church an eternal rest that becomes a wellspring of delight for every believer. Everyone who looks to Christ for salvation has already entered that rest. It is not merely anticipated by marking one day out of the workweek; it is a reality that brings vitality, refreshment, and hope to every day of the week.

One way of putting this, in theological language, is that our leisure (like our work itself) must be viewed *eschatologically*, or by its relation to ultimate things. That is a rather fancy way of saying what Paul said in Colossians: "Set your minds on things above, not on earthly things. For you died, and your life is now hidden with Christ in God. When Christ, who is your life, appears, then you also will appear with him in glory. Put to death, therefore, whatever belongs to your earthly nature: sexual immorality, impurity, lust, evil desires and greed, which is idolatry" (Colossians 3:2–5). The same apostle who had so much to say about the importance of this world—its creation and future redemption and the importance of our involvement in it—nevertheless insisted that we can only be of use to God and to our neighbor if we lock our minds and hearts in on the identity that we have in Christ, since "God raised us up with Christ and seated us with him in the heavenly realms in Christ Jesus" (Ephesians 2:6). We are already seated there theologically, resting in eternal peace.

One cannot help but notice the restlessness of the contemporary Western man or woman, a restlessness that is even obvious (often *most* obvious) during periods of leisure. For a variety of reasons, many will fill those moments with so many diversions, trinkets, toys, and recreations that we often hear, "Now I need a rest from my vacation."

While living in England I realized how much of a child I was myself of this way of thinking. Oxford is a university town, but as university towns go, it is not exactly a Mecca of recreational entertainment. Especially as a native Californian, it took some time for me to get used to the idea that my weekends were going to be spent in the natural pleasures of taking walks and perhaps driving out to a quaint neighboring village pub to meet with friends. My recreation has always been defined by the clutter of toys. J. Gresham Machen, earlier this century, noticed a shift between his generation and the newer one, as children were now growing up *being* entertained, whereas they used to entertain themselves. A baby used to be given a rattle, Machen recalled, but now he is cajoled and showered with toys that will require very little exercise of the child's own imagination and effort.

If only Machen could have seen the computer and arcade games that compete for their market share today! With television, genuine leisure is put at even greater risk. Children and adults discover, after losing their hours like so many grains of sand falling through their fingers, a nagging sense that their time off has not been spent very meaningfully. And yet, we miss it when we do not have it, as I missed the clutter of my amusements while in England.

There is something incredibly sane about a culture that spends its leisure in the most natural, common diversions. It may take some getting used to, but we cannot complain on Monday morning of not really feeling like the weekend was long enough if we are spoiling it with the demand to have other people entertain us rather than entertaining ourselves.

This is a part of what it means to be human. In heaven, God entertains Himself with the communion and fellowship of the triune Godhead, and part of the image of God that we share is a desire for relationships with other people. Most of us are never really happy alone, and that is because we were created for other people; we are not fully ourselves unless we are in communion with a whole range of people and connected by a host of relational bonds. Nevertheless, just as we often require toys to amuse us rather than amusing ourselves with the world God has given us, we are becoming increasingly antisocial and isolated. As the marketplace becomes central in human affairs, making money the object, human relationships are reduced to economic utility. The result of this is that at the end of the day we often feel as if the last thing we want to do is get together with people again.

A word ought to also be said at this point concerning family life. According to many reports, there is a growing concern for carving out space in busy schedules for meaningful family time. Some of my closest friends growing up were Mormons, and one of the most interesting rituals in their week was "Family Home Evening," when (usually on Wednesdays, as I recall) the entire family was expected to be home for games, readings, and other recreations. It must be noted, however, that this is no panacea for family problems. Too often, we find a technique and glorify "family life" in such a way that the realities of sin are not appreciated and are either dismissed as impossible in "such a godly home" as ours or are treated as blemishes on the parents' spiritual pride that often leave little room for the Gospel. Nevertheless, something must be done to improve our family life.

Since the very beginning, the family has been the divine institution closest to God's heart.

A bit closer to home, it used to be the case that the Lord's Day was taken rather seriously. Although one might gather from the discussion above that the Sabbath as an earthly institution no longer exists, since the reality has come in Christ, there is nevertheless every reason to guard the day of public worship as a day of family worship as well. Although the New Testament does not reissue the Sabbath commandment, as early as the apostolic era, Sunday was being celebrated as "the Lord's Day" (Revelation 1:10), because it was the weekly anniversary of Christ's resurrection, the event that inaugurated the Sabbath rest for the people of God.

For nearly two thousand years, then, Christians have regarded the Lord's Day as set apart—as the church's "festival day" or, as the Puritans called it, "the market-day of the soul." On this day, one might say, the body rests while the soul feasts and buys up its meats and fruit to last for the rest of the week. No longer Creation, but the Resurrection, now stands firmly in the center of this day. It is special not because of its location on the calendar, but because it is the day on which, by apostolic authority, the Word was to be preached and the sacraments were to be administered. In other words, the holiness of the activities, not the holiness of the particular day, created "the Lord's Day" and fastened it to the minds, hearts, and imaginations of generations of Christians.

But the Lord's Day has fallen on hard times in Christian circles in our day. While we may justly condemn a legalism that Paul warned against in Colossians 2:16–17, today we have swung to the opposite pole. An argument can easily be made that one of the factors leading to the present condition of the church is that it has scuttled the Lord's Day. Throughout Israel's history, idolatry and desecration of worship went hand in hand: As the people lost an interest in God, they found the gods of the nations more entertaining. Mind you, I am not saying that this is a superstitious fetish and that, if we uphold the Lord's Day, God is bound to bless us. I am saying that there is a very practical, common-sense relationship between the ignorance and apathy of the churches and the lack of seriousness with which they take their ordained mission. Very often, especially in many megachurches today, the real activity of the church goes on during the week, with small groups and functions that are rather low in serious biblical content. Instead of getting unchurched Harry or Mary into the church through recovery groups and parties, they often end up merely converting the rest of the church to recovery groups and parties.

A FAMILY MATTER

Families, therefore, are going to have to take the lead in this matter of restoring the Lord's Day to its splendor. Since the very beginning, the family has been the divine institution closest to God's heart; it is not only the most basic building block of society, but of the church as well. What I am suggesting is the following, with the cavil that this is only a suggestion. You may find an entirely different schedule suited to your distinct needs and pattern, but this is at least a starting point for discussion:

The Lord's Day

Set aside all worldly distractions on Sunday, including sports. This is, I realize, an offensive suggestion to the modern American who has made sports something of an idol, but it is quite possible that the VCR was providentially invented for the express purpose of allowing Christian sports fans to enjoy the game later. Before the service, ask the children to take notes on the sermon; upon returning, perhaps during Sunday dinner, ask each to share his or her notes with the family, and then discuss the content and its applications to the particular situations in which the family finds itself. After dinner, it might be a good idea to take a nap and then enjoy an afternoon activity together. Make it a normal pattern to find family recreations that allow family members to enjoy each other's company: a drive, walk, hike, bicycle ride. Then, return in time for Sunday evening services. It is true that fellowship with other believers at church is an important part of the Lord's Day, but it is secondary to the fellowship between the "little church" that consists of one's own family members.

The Evening Meal

Make the daily evening meal a special time for the family to regroup and discuss the events of the day. In many cases, our children's friends will have a very different pattern and may wonder why our children are expected to be home at a particular hour every night, but in time they may very well want to get their parents to do the same. Regardless, the evening meal is the ideal time to touch bases. In the past, Protestant families made the evening meal the time for brief prayer and the steady memorization of the catechism (a question-and-answer guide to the Bible's main doctrinal themes, especially for children). Looking around the table, the leader of the house would ask each person to recall the question and answer, and then would read the verses listed beside the answer in the catechism. Discussion would follow. This gave generations of Protestants a simple method of training children in the essentials of the Christian faith; this they regarded as primarily their duty and only secondarily the church's.

Family Night

Select a day of the week that can become as routine as the morning newspaper and use this weekday for a "Family Night." Select a good book—perhaps a classic novel, or a collection of poems, short stories, or fairy tales. Break the evening up with a game or some time around the piano or guitar. Perhaps you will want to have Bible study during the same period as well, but it is vital that children grow up also respecting and enjoying secular literature.

Reading Aloud

Be sure to read to your children at their earliest ages. Studies have shown that children whose parents read to them even before they can understand any of the words grow up reading and are better learners.

Over many years of research, family psychologist John Rosemond has amassed scores of reasons for turning off the tube. Even "Sesame Street," he argues, is "anti-educational" since it is passive entertainment. In fact, the much-publicized "A.D.D."—Attention Deficit Disorder—Rosemond attributes to little more than the shortening of the attention span that naturally comes with excessive entertainment. Parents, Rosemond points out, "prefer a genetic 'it couldn't be helped' explanation over a developmental one," but the research now substantiates Rosemond's conclusions. Psychologist Jane Healy, author of *Endangered*

Minds: Why Our Children Don't Think (Simon and Schuster), and Yale's Jerome Singer are now chiming in, arguing that children should not be allowed to watch television until they are literate (eight years old).[9]

*The Reformation legitimized marriage as
an end in itself, as it had liberated the
arts, science, philosophy, and politics.*

When parents read to their children, especially bedtime stories, children often learn to make the association between the warmth and security of parental love and a book, and it is then quite natural to turn instinctively to a book instead of a TV show for that warm and pleasurable feeling that people naturally seek in recreation.

These are simply suggestions, of course, and superficial ones at that. Nevertheless, they do point us in a general direction; and often it is not a lack of interest, but a lack of direction, that keeps families from implementing such programs. The solutions may be surprisingly simple, but they require us to fundamentally alter our affections and lifestyles.

Regardless of what one chooses to do, we must put our families first, even before the church. If after the evening mealtimes, Sunday's routine, and the "Family Night" there is time for small groups, Bible studies, and volunteering for various activities and ministries in the church, so much the better. But all too often families get so wrapped up in church activities, with the children in youth groups and the parents in their own specially designed groups, that little time is left for the family to be together. The case of the child who grew up gradually becoming an agnostic because his father was always involved in "ministry" and his mother was wrapped up in women's groups is multiplied too many times in our day. It is time for us to recover the conviction that our most important ministry is to our own families.

157

GOD'S RULE OVER ALL

We have seen the enormity of the problem and the response of Reformation Christianity to the crisis over work and leisure in its day. We have reviewed the biblical foundation for calling, work, and leisure. One of the most impressive paintings of Luther is not a portrait of the man by himself, but with his family, as they are singing with his guitar accompaniment. "His domestic life," writes one historian, "was an integral part of his confession and public testimony."[10] While the medieval church had seen marriage as less spiritual than devotion to God as a monk, the Reformers all agreed that the Christian home was as sacred as the church itself. This did not mean that they had any illusions about its sinlessness, any more than they had about themselves or the church in general: Families were sinful, and harsh correction and strict conformity could never be counted on to drive out sin in the family any more than it could in the individual heart.

First, the Reformation legitimized marriage as an end in itself, as it had liberated the arts, science, philosophy, and politics for their distinct activities. Marriage no more required religious justification than these other spheres, rooted as it was in Creation. In fact, sexual intercourse in marriage was regarded among these Protestants as acceptable for its own sake—simply for pleasure, apart from the greater end of procreation. Luther and Calvin lamented that every father and mother dreaded the possibility of their children being abused, reminding us that the corruption of our day is nothing new in the history of the world. The home, therefore, became a holy place—not because the people inside were "Ozzie and Harriet," but because within those walls a father was shepherding his little flock by the light of Scripture. Here, children grew up with the Word and with parents who took an active interest in the most mundane and secular activities of daily life. Marriage, once considered by the young Luther to be too physical and sensual rather than spiritual and heavenly minded, was now regarded—like all of these other spheres we have been describing—as godly and noble *in* its very earthiness.

Far from scrupulous about the public image of "the perfect family," Luther's theology made such charades repulsive, and he was very open about the normal character of his family life, even calling his wife, "My Lord Kate" in public. "I must have patience with the Pope, ranters, insolent nobles, my household, and Katie von Bora, so that my whole life is nothing else but mere patience," he once declared. Writing to his friend Spalatin, a former superior in the monastery who, having joined the Reformation, now himself recently married, Luther remarked, "When you have your Catherine in bed, sweetly embracing and kissing her, think: Lo, this being, this best little creation of God, has been given me by Christ, to whom be glory and honor. . . . My rib and I send greetings to you and your rib. Grace be with you. Amen." One is struck by the mingling of earthiness and piety. It is not without reason that historians have regularly regarded Luther as the most powerful influence in shaping the distinctives of the Protestant family.

In our day, the relationships between employer and employee, management and labor, husband and wife, parents and children, and work and leisure are all disintegrating. We have observed some of the reasons, and undoubtedly there are others, such as the rampant egalitarianism that regards any hierarchy or order of authority as inherently malicious. But Scripture does not teach us to level all relationships and democratize all offices and stations in this world; rather, it calls us to regard our superiors and inferiors with dignity and respect, bringing all of life under the sovereign rule of our Redeemer-King.

One day, a gentleman on a walk passed a construction site and inquired of the workers, "What are you doing?" "I'm breaking rock out of the quarry," said one. Another replied, "I'm in charge of making the mortar that will cement the stones." A third man, caked in mud, was pushing a wheelbarrow, and he stopped just long enough to say, with a sense of proud delight, "I'm building a cathedral." What are we doing with our lives? Working for the weekend or building a cathedral? All three men were engaged in the same task, but only one had the "big picture" in view. Apart from the transcendent (divine, vertical, theological) perspective, we can only see the details of daily routines: I record accounting information, I clean the house, I try cases in court, I type correspondence and make phone calls for other people, and so on. But when we begin to sign the compositions of our daily scores with "Soli Deo Gloria"—"To God Alone Be Glory"—as did Bach, that can make even drudgery divine.

NOTES

1. Leland Ryken, *Work and Leisure in Christian Perspective* (Downers Grove, Ill.: InterVarsity, 1987), 11.

2. Charles A. Reich, *The Greening of America* (New York: Bantam, 1971), 4–7.

3. Ibid., 7.

4. Ibid., 8.

5. From Jacques Ellul's prolific writings to David Wells's *God in the Wasteland: The Reality of God in a World of Fading Dreams* (Grand Rapids: Eerdmans, 1994).

6. Reich, *The Greening of America,* 21.

7. Cited by David Gress, "The Disorder of American Society: Daniel Bell's Cultural Analysis," in *The World & I: A Chronicle of Our Changing Era,* May 1990.

8. John Calvin, *Institutes,* 3.11.6.

9. "Does Constant TV Watching Inhibit Brain Development?", a report by John Rosemond for the Knight-Ridder Newspapers, September 1994.

10. See Steven Ozment, *When Fathers Ruled: Family Life in Reformation Europe* (Cambridge: Harvard Univ., 1983).

Chapter Eight

■

A WORLD
GONE
CRAZY

■

The human tendency is for each generation to regard itself as the center of history; either fame or infamy will serve this craving for historical significance. No age has been as wicked, as vicious, as godless and hopeless as ours, we are often told—as if the invention of more sophisticated means of carrying out the evil in our hearts has somehow deluded us into thinking that human nature alters significantly from age to age.

In spite of the dangers of exaggerated lamentations, there can be little question that the twentieth century has seen some of the most savage brutality and rank evil in all human history. Two World Wars, international terrorism in the form of totalitarianism and fascism, selfish individualism, nationalism, and "the will to power"—one need not rehearse the outline of the century in order to reach a consensus between liberal and conservative alike that it has not been a winning century. Not to be lightly dismissed is the coincidence of these trends in world history and a naked rejection of God.

Evangelical theologian David Wells has chosen to speak of the age in which we live as simply "Our Time." It is a good phrase, particularly because the dust has not settled in the intellectual community concerning the exact nature of the period in which we are now living. In the sixties, the youth rebelled not against Christianity per se (remember, it was one of the most fruitful periods of revival among hippies), but against *modernity*. To whatever extent the churches reflected and defended the structures of modernity, to that extent they were reacting against the churches as well.

One of the problems we Christians make in this business of analyzing and offering critiques of our culture is to look always on the surface of things. Because we may be able to recall the confrontations on university campuses and reports on the evening news, our log of images leads us to the conclusion that the rebellion of that period was the problem rather than a symptom. Today we still commit the same fallacy, viewing elections as momentous, epoch-making events. If our candidate is elected, his or her victory is often met with lavish and hyperbolic expressions that would have perhaps even made Napoleon blush. By contrast, if the rascal made it into office, letters roll off the presses of Christian organizations that will become next week's lamentation from evangelical pulpits across the land: The forces of evil have triumphed, sin is now firmly entrenched, and the good people (like ourselves) are exiled. One might have thought that we had passed into an entirely new age due to the most recent elections. That was not only true in the last elections; it has been true for a long time, because we are caught up in the trivial and bored by that which is truly significant and history-making.

If the United States were invaded by foreign armies and it ceased to exist as a sovereign state, in all likelihood there would be enormous economic, social, international, political, and military ramifications, but unlike the Greco-Roman empires, the United States (for all of its international influence) has tended to spread its popular culture rather than its high culture. Although one may be able to find American soft drinks in the most remote native village of the Andes and children wearing L.A. Raiders T-shirts while chasing a ball in the streets of Damascus, will historians five centuries hence be able to unearth the deeper cultural influences of America's ascendancy and worldwide prominence?

I am not saying that the daily news is unimportant or that the things that go on in popular culture are irrelevant. What I am saying is that unless we understand the deeper trends in intellectual culture, we are going to be caught off guard every time we show up at the scene of the crime. In past ages, Christians have played a significant role not only in figuring out where we were on the philosophical and historical map, but in actually contributing to the ideas and events that redraw the chart. They did this because they were called to do it as human beings, but they also did it because they wanted to fulfill Christ's command to be "fishers of men." Some fishermen stand on the banks of a calm pond, waiting for a strike. Others cast nets, in expansive evangelistic campaigns. But still others are to be found throughout history wading chest-deep into the powerful stream of human thought, refusing to be swept along by the current, but determined to bring in a significant catch. One type of fishing is not to be trumpeted to the exclusion of the others, but as Christian and non-Christian thinkers have pointed out rather relentlessly, evangelical Christianity has avoided these formidable mountain rivers for some time.

Whether our activities, however vigorous, will be able to turn the tide of the intellectual community and restrain secularism is a divine secret to which we have not been made privy. But there can be no doubt that, in spite of the results, Christian duty absolutely requires us to recover our interest in the deeper questions that once ruled the hearts and minds of our forebears.

To that end, we will briefly summarize "Our Time" in terms of its major currents and suggest some possible avenues of making more meaningful contributions to the world in this time and place.

MODERNITY: WHEN WAS IT?

Here one is likely to encounter a wide range of opinion. For instance, Thomas Oden argues that the age of modernity began with the storming of the Bastille in 1789 and ended with the collapse of the Berlin Wall in 1989. Historians have normally regarded the division of "modern history" as beginning with the Renaissance and Reformation, but only recently have they begun offering theories as to when (or if) it has come to an end. For reasons I shall defend below, I would argue that "modernity," rooted in the Renaissance and the Enlightenment, has not come to an end at all and that even its most relentless secular critics often betray a radically "modern" outlook in their very attack on "modernity."

MODERNITY: WHAT IS IT?

Augustine once said that he knew what time was until someone asked him to define it. The same is true with "modernity." It has become a ubiquitous term in academic discourse and has just now filtered down to the masses as it appears in daily newspapers on occasion.

Briefly summarized, most scholars concur that modernity possesses the following features:

Belief in Progress

In the Renaissance (14th–16th centuries), the new intellectuals were eager to return to a supposed "Golden Age" of civilization, located in ancient Greece and Rome. Convinced that they were living in a barren period of ecclesiastical dogmatism and obsession with the status quo, many Renaissance figures were inspired by the histories, poetry, art, languages, and philosophies of the ancient world. It was these young intellectuals and artists who coined the phrase "dark ages" in referring to the period between the fall of Rome and their own careers! (No age has been without its hubris.) In the Middle Ages, an imaginative monk by the name of Joachim of Fiore wrote a commentary on the book of Revelation in which he asserted that humanity was on the brink of something remarkable. Just as the Age of the Father (Old Testament) had passed to the greater Age of the Son (New Testament), the world was about to enter the apex of civilization in the Age of the Spirit. In this new age, all religions would be united as dogma would retreat in the presence of spiritual brotherhood and unity. (One can faintly hear John Lennon's "Imagine" in the background.) Understandably, the Roman church forbade Jo-achim's heretical interpretation of history, but it made an impression on many Renaissance leaders, especially those who were attempting to unite faintly Christian theology to a fundamentally pagan Neoplatonic mysticism. A brilliant star in this constellation was Petrarch, and it was he, more than anyone else, who secularized the thought of the banned monk for an age that was convinced it was entering a new era of enlightenment.

A Neoplatonist himself, Petrarch believed that spirit was superior to matter. Instead of going all the way with this Greek mysticism by arguing that salvation meant the spirit's escape from its physical "prison-house," he followed Joachim's vision, insisting that history itself was moving beyond material existence (church, sacraments, Bible, creed, doctrine) and entering a spiritual epoch. Sir Thomas More's *Utopia* points up this anticipation that held the epoch's greatest minds under its spell. The Anabaptists at the time of the Reformation adopted this approach and anticipated the imminent advent of the Holy Spirit to bring the world into a state of perfect peace and holiness. In fact, a radical Anabaptist sect sought to usher in this Age of the Spirit by force, taking over the German city of Munster and turning it into a communist, polygamous state from which perfectionistic revolutions would emanate throughout the world. Although most Anabaptists were less revolutionary, their radical dualism between matter and spirit led them to despise this world and forbid involvement in its affairs.

This idea of progress eventually led a number of influential scientists and philosophers of science to divorce their discipline from the "superstitions" and "dogmas" of faith.

The plot thickens with the arrival on the scene of the German Enlightenment philosopher, G. W. F. Hegel (1770–1831). Hegel advanced this view of history in a philosophy of pantheism (all is "God"). History itself was the progress toward this perfect state of pure spirit, and since all of history, like all of spiritual existence, is one, this progress itself is synonymous with "God." Out of this pantheistic mysticism, combined with a rigorous rationalism, Hegel developed his famous dialectic: History was now viewed as a spiral toward perfect spiritual perfection through thesis, antithesis, and synthesis. One can see how this actually looks in real life with the arrival of the next character in this saga: Karl Marx (1818–83).

Regarding Hegel as his philosophical father and the Anabaptist revolutionaries as precursors, Marx was convinced that his "spiritual secularism," or "secular spiritualism," as we might call it, would lead to the anticipated utopia. For that reason, Marx could even approve of feudalism in the Middle Ages as a "thesis" requiring the "antithesis" of the peasant's revolt in the sixteenth century, leading finally to a "synthesis" that was one step closer to the realization of utopia. Marx even considered democracy an important and positive stage toward the "new age," just as he believed that totalitarianism would have to be a brief but necessary evil toward the attainment of his perfect society. Hegel's philosophy is everywhere evident: Totalitarianism is not the goal, but the means of attaining its very antithesis—the elimination of the state and perfect peace and harmony. The perfect state is achieved not in a direct line, but by zigzagging from successive reactions and counter-reactions. This is why one can still find hard-core Marxists (almost always to be found in American university and seminary faculties) who view the "collapse" of Soviet Marxism as nothing more than a necessary "antithesis" in the inevitable progress of history. There is a "blind faith" commitment to the deterministic notion that history has the Marxist vision as its goal, even though there is no such thing as an intelligent Creator who determines history!

But Marx was not alone in his debt to Hegel and this modern vision of progress. In fact, Hegel was as much the father of capitalism as of communism, in that Adam Smith (author of *The Wealth of Nations*, which was so instrumental in the rise of industrial capitalism) depended on his view of historical progress as well. It was the vision that inspired John Dewey, father of modern education; Sigmund Freud, father of psychology; and Friederich Schleiermacher, father of modern theological liberalism. This idea of progress eventually led a number of influential scientists and philosophers of science to divorce their discipline from the "superstitions" and "dogmas" of faith, advancing the notion that to be a man or woman of faith was to be "backward-looking," whereas the scientific outlook (i.e., the naturalistic outlook) was marching arm-and-arm with progress. Charles Darwin was merely a child of his Hegelian age when he advanced a theory that explained natural history in terms of evolutionary progress. Was his theory actually justified by the facts of scientific inquiry, or was it a philosophical speculation that just "happened" to coincide with Marxian and similar attempts to explain every facet of human life according to Hegel's speculative opinions?

As with all cursory summaries, this one is reductionistic. For instance, Hegel was certainly not the single-handed architect of modernity and its view of progress. It was a universal dogma of the Enlightenment that as "enlightened" men and women took their eyes off the past and its religious dogmas, eventually the morning would dawn and the world would achieve its final peace.

Added to these intellectual trends was the remarkable explosion in technology. The Industrial Revolution gave these paragons of progress the machine, and it seemed that "nothing would be impossible for them." Technology gave material shape to the spirit of progress, and the general bent of philosopher and shopkeeper alike was toward the future, as people became increasingly convinced that advances in science, medicine, education, politics, the behavioral sciences, and so forth would achieve utopia. No wonder, then, that utopian political movements threw the last two centuries into convulsion, from both the right and the left. Utopia's advent could even justify the slaughter of millions who stood in the way of the "illumined ones." In spite of all of the atrocities committed in the name of Christendom, nothing ever attempted in Christ's name even approximated the dogmatism, oppression, and superstition of the modern world.

Universal Reason

David Hume (1711–76) was a British empiricist who insisted that whatever could not be observed could not be considered "knowledge." Unlike the rationalists, who said that they knew something was true because it conformed to universal principles of reason, the empiricists said that they knew something was true because it conformed to universal experience and observation. Since Hume believed that miracles are not part of universal experience or observation, they must be ruled out *a priori* as a possibility in a universe that operates strictly according to natural laws. Christ's resurrection, therefore, could not have happened— not because the facts of the case are overwhelmingly opposed to it, but because resurrections are, by definition, miraculous, and miracles cannot occur in the universe that we know to exist.

That which begins today as a philosophical speculation ends up moving armies and building empires tomorrow.

Immanuel Kant (1724–1804) reduced the field of that which can legitimately be known to rationalism. Universal principles of reason exist within every mind, and it is these principles that must lead us to our conclusions about the world. Nevertheless, Kant was awakened from his "dogmatic slumbers" in rationalism by Hume's radical empiricism, and he attempted to blend these two philosophical schools. Therefore, faith was in the "noumenal" (spiritual) realm of that which cannot be demonstrated to reason or observation, while science and philosophy belonged to the rational and observable realm (i.e., the *phenomenal* realm). The only "facts" of religion that could be demonstrated were those of natural reason. In this way Kant, reared in pietism, reduced the realm of rational religion to morality. After all, the "universal principles" of morality are evident in even the most uncivilized cultures. At the end of the day, however, Kant insisted that all human knowledge is subjective. That is, one never does see things "as they are," but must necessarily construct "reality" according to these principles of universal reason. Thus, if one has already concluded by argument and reason that something cannot be true, it cannot be *demonstrated* as true even by obvious evidence or testimony. All human observation is "interpreted" by reason, so that the subject (the knower) rather than the object (that which is known) is the source of true knowledge.

Thus, the entire Enlightenment project was dedicated to the building of a tower of progress reaching to the heavens. It was a secular spiritualism, a naturalistic religion of human achievement with little or no place for God, much less for His revelation or redemption. Linked to the dogma of inevitable progress, modernity championed the omnipotence of human reason to understand everything necessary and to solve every theoretical and practical problem standing in the way of progress.

WHAT WERE THE PRACTICAL RESULTS?

That which begins today as a philosophical speculation ends up moving armies and building empires tomorrow. We have seen the practical effects of modernity in the revolutions of the last two and a half centuries. It has had the tendency of centralizing power in cities and in powerful governmental centers. In the past, a healthy culture has required strong families, neighborhoods, schools, and churches, and, only after these primary institutions, good national governments. But in our day, just as the suburban mall has replaced the shop, federal government and the statism that it produces often render these more immediate, personal, and meaningful centers of gravity irrelevant to our lives. But we also see the effects in our everyday lives, in ways that often elude us simply because they have become so much a part of our world that we take them for granted.

Let me use some examples. Very often human existence and nature is described in quite mechanical terms, as if man were simply an advanced machine determined by natural processes, just as we might program a computer. The uniqueness of human existence and the freedom of human action is often called into question even in our everyday life, as criminals are regarded as "products" of their society, for instance. Apartment complexes, condominium or townhouse buildings, and the like are erected around the shrines of modern business and industry. Even our neighborhoods—if we can still call them that—are increasingly becoming memorials to modernity. Especially in the postwar period, modernity and its effects (technology, especially rapid travel) have uprooted us from our ancestral places and given us a feeling of impermanence and superficiality. Instead of a community, with the pride of generations building material and spiritual tributes, we have the modern "tract homes," planned communities in which buildings of artificial material pop up like tents almost overnight. In spite of diverse floorplans, each house looks similar and occupies roughly the same amount of land. Our mobility is increasingly producing a rootless culture that, by definition, cannot take as much pride in place and time as that enjoyed by previous generations. Fast-food franchises even cluster around these "neighborhoods," capitalizing on the fact that, in our frantic lives, we no longer expect dinner to be an opportunity for family and friends to gather for community. Friendships and families fracture more easily in this environment, but we often fail to see into this situation more deeply than the obvious moral and political policies of "family values."

The telecommunications revolution has also radically altered the relational landscape. Until rather recently, some European countries refused to conduct official government business by phone, since the slower, more formal, and less direct method of letters has the tendency to limit misunderstandings and the immediacy of hot tempers flaring. I even notice a difference in communication between friends in England and in America. Like most Americans, I tend to rush through my communication with friends, family members, and colleagues, selecting the most rapid form of communication and taking the least amount of time to cover the necessary ground. By contrast, almost all of my English friends correspond with me in longhand, written letters. The penmanship is remarkable, especially compared to mine; I joked to a friend about this, only to learn that he took penmanship more seriously than I took it. It was no joke. Beyond the appearance, the content is more meaningful, both in terms of its depth and style of writing. It is not simply the cost of a phone call that accounts for this, as it is a common form of communication even between people living in the same community. Is it not at least possible that these two different patterns in communication tend to create two distinct approaches to relationships?

In the late twenties, when radio was just beginning to enjoy popular success, the orthodox Protestant leader J. Gresham Machen lamented the effects that this would have on culture. First, he observed that his students were finding it difficult to read or enjoy their leisure in natural pastimes but required noise to soothe them. Second, he warned that it would help to produce a banal popular culture in which local cultures gave way to a homogeneous style of music that would dull taste and destroy individuality. Like the tract homes, television (far more than radio) has helped to create this homogenous popular culture in which the mob mentality undercuts our ability to entertain ourselves and to think and create for ourselves. A mass-produced (and therefore superficial) "world" is served up to us in a deluge of images and sounds. Our foreign brothers and sisters are often offended when they enter our homes, only to find us carrying on conversations in a "living room" in which the furniture is arranged around the ubiquitous blue-screen icon. It is not the existence of such appliances that offends them, but the prominence that we give them in our lives. It is not uncommon for Christian families to arrange more than their furniture—their very lives—around television, so that it is on even during meals and conversations. Many of the people who protest the sex and violence in the media do not seem to have the slightest concern over the deeper and more significant long-term impact of television. It is not only the message (which is a constant stream of modernity's deepest convictions packaged for mass consumption), but the medium itself, that causes us to question its prominence in our lives and in our culture.

Note what I am not saying at this point. I am not suggesting for one moment that we should eschew apartment buildings, snobbishly frown on tract homes (I live in one of the ugliest), make a pact to live in one place for the rest of our lives, boycott hamburger joints, and resolve to communicate with our friends and colleagues by letter rather than by phone or fax. I do not think it is sinful to own a TV set or to go to movies. (After all, I have included some illustrations from films in this book!) Like everything else, we simply have to be discerning and thoughtful. We cannot go back, and we should not wish to become cultural dinosaurs. Nevertheless, we must realize the enormous ramifications of modernity (both good and bad) in our own lives if we are to seek to compensate for its negative effects.[1]

WHERE WERE THE EVANGELICALS IN ALL OF THIS?

The label "evangelical" came into use during the Reformation. Luther, Calvin, and other Reformers led evangelical Christianity at a time when the modern world was coming into being. A wide consensus of historical scholarship attests to the fact that a great many of the advances in science, the arts and letters, politics, and society in general were products of the Reformation. This is not cut-and-dried, as there was often a mixture of secular and religious ideas dominating the period. Nevertheless, as we have seen in previous chapters, the Reformation launched mighty projects in human culture. The idolaters of the modern age often fail to take into account the extent to which their dreams could not have been apart from the dream of biblical Christianity. Even their secular vision of progress was based on the Christian eschatology of redemption and hope. The project of declaring independence from God—that is, of repeating the Fall—itself requires Christianity to be true.

We ourselves must see to it that we are the church—the body of Christ—again in our age.

The devoted religionists of modernity have convinced generations of men and women that Christianity was responsible for everything that is wrong in the modern world. Environmental neglect was the result of a Christian view of the world in which human beings dominated the rest of creation, as sexism was the result of the patriarchal paradigm of Judeo-Christian culture. Racism, violence, and a host of other modern plagues have been attributed so relentlessly to Christianity that society has come to accept the blame as given.

Our response in the midst of all this ought not to be merely reactionary.[2] It is true that Christianity has been exploited even by theologians and ministers in the service of left-wing and right-wing ideology; they have surrendered to the various Baals of modernity, using Christianity as a cloak for racism, exploitation of the environment, slavery, sexism, technology, and the worship of power. We must recognize this, repent of it, and turn again to Yahweh, the one true God of history who has made Himself known in the person and work of Christ. Before we can expect unbelievers to do this, we ourselves must see to it that we are the church—the body of Christ—again in our age.

In spite of the complex factors that continue to disturb our world and disintegrate our relationships, we know that history will meet its appointed end, that God "has set a day when he will judge the world with justice by the man he has appointed. He has given proof of this to all men by raising him from the dead" (Acts 17:31). God is still sovereign, ruling in the affairs of all people, the high and the low, the powerful and the weak. Regardless of who occupies the White House, Congress, or the Supreme Court, "His dominion is an eternal dominion; his kingdom endures from generation to generation. All the peoples of the earth are regarded as nothing. He does as he pleases with the powers of heaven and the peoples of the earth. No one can hold back his hand or say to him: 'What have you done?'" (Daniel 4:34–35). Even after all the great empires have come and gone, God will still be carrying out His plans, made before the creation of the world, to glorify Himself in the salvation of the elect and in the judgment of the damned.

It is this realization that produces hope. But it is not a sentimentalized hope based on a romantic view of God and a platitudinous belief that "everything will work out"; it is a hope that realizes that salvation and "utopia" will be finally realized not by human striving, but by the intervention of justice at the end of the age. Then the new heavens and the new earth will be bound together into one splendid Eden, with no serpent to spoil the arrangement. In one instant, we will be glorified, and our only delight will be to serve God and our neighbor. Of the heavenly city, we read, "On no day will its gates ever be shut, for there will be no night there. The glory and honor of the nations will be brought into it. Nothing impure will ever enter it, nor will anyone who does what is shameful or deceitful, but only those whose names are written in the Lamb's book of life" (Revelation 21:25–27). Even as we work for real change and actively pursue our calling in this world, we cry out in our deep distress, "Even so, Lord, come quickly!"

NOTES

1. For excellent treatments of the influence of technology see Neil Postman, *Technopoly* (New York: Knopf, 1993); Jacques Ellul, *The Humiliation of the Word* (Grand Rapids: Eerdmans, 1985).
2. Additional studies of the postmodern condition include *The Condition of Postmodernity,* by David Harvey (Oxford: Blackwell, 1989) and, from a Christian perspective, especially the following: Roger Lundin, *The Culture of Interpretation* (Grand Rapids: Eerdmans, 1992); Thomas Oden, *After Modernity . . . What?* (Grand Rapids: Zondervan, 1992); Gene E. Veith, Jr., *Postmodern Times* (Wheaton, Ill.: Crossway, 1994).

Conclusion:

∎

IN THE WORLD BUT NOT OF IT

∎

The joys of the world hinder spiritual joy to the greatest degree and make minds incapable of it. Worldly joy is gross, spiritual joy is subtle. Worldly joy draws man into the flesh, spiritual joy lifts him. Worldly joy puts him ill at ease, spiritual joy gives him peace."[1]

The author of the preceding was Philipp Jakob Spener, regarded as the father of "pietism," a movement within the Protestant churches of seventeenth-century Germany that attempted to recover what its adherents believed to be a balance between sound doctrine and sound living. Raised in orthodox Lutheran and Reformed churches, the pietists were concerned that so many could answer all the questions of the catechism with great accuracy, yet could display little effect of such truth in their lives. The heart was cold, the hands unemployed in acts of Christian piety, they asserted with great skill and passion.

Today, "pietism" has become a shibboleth for an inward piety that ignores the world, except as a target for evangelism and missions. While such caricatures ignore the wealth of insight from these energetic and zealous followers of Christ, there is a marked difference between the world-affirming theology of the Reformers and the generally world-denying outlook of the pietists. At the time of the Reformation itself, the Protestant Reformers faced not only the abuses of Rome, but the excesses of the Anabaptists who wanted to separate entirely from the world.

Scripture teaches us that there are two dangers to avoid— separatism and worldliness—and church history teaches us how easily we fall into either. In the ancient church, Justin Martyr was so wrapped up in philosophy that even after his conversion he saw Christianity as essentially a philosophical system and incorporated incompatible Greek ideas into Christianity. Tertullian, on the other hand, insisted that Christianity and philosophy are so opposed that there is no common ground. In the Middle Ages, by contrast, the church had synthesized Greek philosophy and Scripture so that one could not question the former without casting doubt on the latter. But the Anabaptists responded by repudiating involvement in the world altogether, and the pietists who followed the period of the Reformation showed many of the same signs. Although the Reformers were not infallible, they did liberate Christian theology from philosophy, while affirming both, and gave each room in which to breathe.

Let us then hold each of these views up to the light of Scripture for analysis.

THE BIBLICAL DOCTRINE
OF CREATION: IN THE WORLD

As we have seen, the Bible stands diametrically opposed to any view, Greek or otherwise, that downplays the reality or importance of the created world. It is not only that God pronounced the world good in the beginning, but it is *in* that world that God announced His plan of redemption after the Fall and executed it in real history. It was through the Red Sea, not a mythical, "spiritual" river of eternal life, that God saved Israel from Pharaoh's army. It was at a real mountain in the ancient Near East that God gave His people the Law and led them through the wilderness.

The wilderness was not dreary and sad because it was *earthly,* but because it was not the *Promised Land*—the "land flowing with milk and honey." God was worshiped in a real temple, with real sacrifices of living animals.

The Gospel writers underscored Christ's humanity by appealing to His human genealogy. His ancestors were real human beings—some people of outstanding character, others diabolical, and most reflecting both tendencies in their lives—according to the biblical record. In other words, redemption, according to the Bible, is "earthed" in real time and space history, unlike other religions which seem to share a common dualism between that which is "spiritual" (i.e., heavenly) and that which is "evil" (i.e., earthly). Even non-Christians, according to Scripture, possess the image of God (James 3:9) and are, therefore, just as capable as Christians of excellence, wisdom and knowledge in things of this world, creativity, pleasure, and civil virtue.

Against all who would say that the earth belongs to Satan or evil forces, God Himself announces, "The world is mine, and all that is in it" (Psalm 50:12). He created it and upholds it by His power. Even in its present state of rebellion, His common grace brings good out of evil and restrains human wickedness. "He sends rain on the righteous and the unrighteous," and that is meant to lead us to imitate God's generosity toward unbelievers (Matthew 5:45).

THE BIBLICAL DOCTRINE
OF REDEMPTION: BUT NOT OF THE WORLD

If all this is true, why does John tell us that we must "not love the world or anything in the world" (1 John 2:15)? Surely John cannot mean "the world" in a general sense, since he was the same apostle who declared, "For God so loved the world, that he gave his only begotten Son" (John 3:16 KJV). What John intends here is "the world" in its fallenness, in its hostility to God and opposition to His Word.

It is because the earth and all that is in it belongs to the Lord that He can—indeed, must—judge it because of its rebellion. "I will punish the world for its evil," He declares (Isaiah 13:11). But the redemption is as thorough as the judgment. I have found it interesting that many Christians have no trouble recognizing that the final judgment of sinners includes the judgment of the world. Fire, devastation, destruction will come to creation. This is something that we hear a great deal about, especially from those who commit themselves to trying to predict the end. And yet, that is no more the whole story of what happens to the earth than it is the whole story of what happens to humanity. It is not only a redeemed *people* that God has in store, but a redeemed *creation:* "The creation waits in eager expectation for the sons of God to be revealed. For the creation was subjected to frustration, not by its own choice, but by the will of the one who subjected it, in hope that the creation itself will be liberated from its bondage to decay and brought into the glorious freedom of the children of God. We know that the whole creation has been groaning as in the pains of childbirth right up to the present time" (Romans 8:19–22). Paul follows that great announcement with the declaration that our own bodies will one day be redeemed as part of this redemption of creation (v. 23).

In Christianity, religion is a matter
of history, not just of the heart.
It is true whether we believe it or not.

The gnostic views redemption in terms of salvation *from* the body, material existence, time, history, and this world; the biblical writers in both Old and New Testaments describe salvation in terms of salvation *of* the body and soul together *in* time, history, and this world. The cross was a real scaffold made of real wood. The Crucifixion occurred, along with the Resurrection, during a real week in history. It was not the inner experience of His disciples in their hearts that is recorded in Scripture for our saving faith, but that "which we have heard, which we have seen with our eyes, which we have looked at and our hands have touched—this we proclaim concerning the Word of life" (1 John 1:1). In

Christianity, religion is a matter of history, not just of the heart. It is true whether we believe it or not.

This world is not the Christian's enemy, then, *as the world.* In other words, it is not our humanness or the world in its essence that is the problem. Skewed by the gnostic influence, many Christians speak of their remaining sinfulness as if it were directly linked to their humanness: "As long as we have this fleshly body, we are going to be held back from our perfect, spiritual existence," expresses such sentiments. But as Calvin put it, when arguing against the gnostics of his day, "It is not nature, but the corruption of nature" that is at issue. This is what we must get straight if we are going to be world-affirming in our spirituality.

Nevertheless, we cannot escape the other side of the coin that we find throughout Scripture. If the Bible is opposed to the pagan dualisms between spirit and matter and is affirming of this world, it is also opposed to *worldliness.* Worldly activity is not only sanctioned by God, but commanded. But *worldliness* is the disease of the soul that infects us when we begin to pattern our ideas, beliefs, methods, and lifestyles according to the world. Many of us grew up in churches where this "worldliness" was associated with secular callings, financial success, and dancing, drinking, smoking, or hanging around people and places where these activities took place. This is *not*—emphatically, *not*—the worldliness described by Scripture. We become worldly when "Phil Donahue" pep talks replace sermons, worship is transformed for market-driven consumerism, and therapeutic or political categories begin to replace the solid biblical emphasis in our churches. We become worldly when obsessions with "practical" issues replace well-informed discipleship and when we begin to think that visible popularity and numerical success are the measures of ministry.

It is quite possible to be thoroughly corrupted by worldliness even while we are safely tucked away in the Christian ghetto. Our Christian music, literature, schools, broadcasting, and churches can themselves be carriers of the virus of worldliness without ever having to bother with the world.

Like the vessels in the Old Testament sanctuary that had been set aside from ordinary use to sacred use, believers are "vessels of mercy, which He prepared beforehand for glory" (Romans 9:23 NASB). This is not something to which we must attain, as if holiness were dependent on the extent to which we set ourselves apart from the world. Rather, God has taken all of the burden upon Himself for this: By sending the Holy One of Israel to be our substitute, to live a sinless life of perfect conformity to His Father's revealed will, and to go to the cross to bear our sins; and then by raising Him from the dead for our justification, God's holiness and justice were completely satisfied. Like the Prodigal Son, we wear robes of righteousness which our Father has placed over our nakedness at great personal cost. In Adam, we are guilty and corrupt, but in Christ we are holy and blameless, without spot or wrinkle. "It is because of him that you are in Christ Jesus, who has become for us wisdom from God—that is, our righteousness, holiness and redemption," and this excludes all boasting in our own pretended holiness (1 Corinthians 1:30–31).

This is called "definitive sanctification," because it is a once-and-for-all declaration in God's courtroom that defines who we are right now. It is not the degree of holiness that we have attained or will attain that brings us close to God, but the perfect holiness of Christ that gives us our status and qualifies us to enter the Holy of Holies.

The Bible does not stop there, however. Not only has He clothed us in Christ's righteousness and holiness, imputing Christ's thirty-three years of perfect obedience; He has also toppled the unholy trinity—the world, the flesh, and the devil—from their tyrannical throne. The triumphant indicative (the declaration that we already *are* holy in Christ) is followed by the imperative (the command to live in a manner that is consistent with that fact). Our status before God (the indicative) is never dependent upon our progress in personal holiness (the imperative), but both belong to every genuine believer. However slight the progress in godliness in the course of this life, there is progress; and however much sin still clings to the justified sinner, he or she is still wearing the robe of Christ's perfect holiness.

Once we get that distinction straight, we are liberated to pursue godliness out of reverence and gratitude rather than out of fear of punishment and a selfish hope for personal reward. It also keeps us from the opposite dangers of perfectionism and quietism: We work with energetic activity in the world, without illusions of perfection until we stand before God in glory. It is the good news of the indicative (what God has done in Christ) that keeps us going even in spite of our failures to rise to the imperative challenges.

Peter also follows this order in his first epistle. First, we have the indicative: "Praise be to the God and Father of our Lord Jesus Christ! In his great mercy he *has given us* new birth into a living hope through the resurrection of Jesus Christ from the dead, and into an inheritance that can never perish, spoil or fade—*kept in heaven* for you, who through faith *are shielded* by God's power until the coming of the salvation that is ready to be revealed in the last time" (1 Peter 1:3–5). In other words, the holiness that makes us acceptable to God is already ours in Christ, objectively, by grace alone through faith alone. And then Peter follows this with the imperative: "Therefore, *prepare your minds* for action; be self-controlled; *set your hope* fully on the grace to be given you when Jesus Christ is revealed. As obedient children, *do not conform* to the evil desires you had when you lived in ignorance. But just as he who called you is holy, so *be holy* in all you do; for it is written: 'Be holy, because I am holy'" (vv. 13–16). We are to live in this world "as strangers here in reverent fear," because "you know that it was not with perishable things such as silver or gold that you were redeemed from the empty way of life handed down to you from your forefathers, but with the precious blood of Christ, a lamb without blemish or defect" (vv. 17–19). We were "purified" through faith in Christ and "have been born again, not of perishable seed, but of imperishable, through the living and enduring word of God" (vv. 22–23).

Peter returns to this pattern of indicative and imperative in the next chapter. Beginning with Christ as God's temple in whom we all fit as "living stones," Peter does not hold this out as a possibility for "victorious, fully consecrated Christians" at the end of their Christian lives, but declares that it is a present reality for every believer. "But you *are* a chosen people, a royal priesthood, a holy nation, a people belonging to God, *that you may declare* the praises of him who called you out of darkness into his wonderful light" (2:9). In other words, this gracious act of God has a point: We are not saved by grace alone in order to live to ourselves, but in order to glorify God. Therefore, "Dear friends, I urge you, as aliens and strangers in the world, to abstain from sinful desires, which war against your soul. Live such good lives among the pagans that, though they accuse you of doing wrong, they may see your good deeds and glorify God on the day he visits us" (vv. 11–12).

At the price of Christ's own blood, we were purchased by God. The imagery here in 1 Peter 1:3–4 belongs to the world of commerce and specifically to the world of slavery. In the Greco-Roman world, slavery was usually economic: A debtor would fulfill his obligations by serving his creditor. Other slaves were foreigners carried off as booty in wartime victories. Similarly, we were the slaves of unrighteousness. The world, the flesh, and the devil controlled our worldview, our attitudes, and our motivations. Although they might promise perks in the short run, slavery to sin leads to death. Peter describes Jesus as a man at an auction, bidding on the slaves in the city square. Sin, death, hell, and the world all placed high bids on us, but no one and nothing could outbid Christ's price: His own blood.

But we were freed not to belong to ourselves; we are now under new ownership.

This was the point our Lord made in His High Priestly Prayer: Believers "are not of the world any more than I am of the world. My prayer is not that you take them out of the world but that you protect them from the evil one. They are not of the world, even as I am not of it. Sanctify them by the truth; your word is truth. As you sent me into the world, I have sent them into the world. For them I sanctify myself, that they too may be truly sanctified" (John 17:14–19).

Notice the important point Jesus makes here. First, the indicative: We are sanctified (holy, set apart) not because we have progressively separated ourselves from the world, but because Christ separated Himself from the world and we are in Christ. But because that is true of us all, we must *recognize* and *respond to* this fact by progressively extricating ourselves from the worldly perspective and the character it produces. We never do accomplish this fully in our earthly lives, but it is the goal toward which we zealously strive.

WHAT DOES THIS MEAN
FOR A CHRISTIAN WORLDVIEW?

Given this picture of creation and redemption, what applications can we make for our own lives at work and play?

Creation and Redemption—
Distinct, but Not Separate

In the beginning, everything was good. After all, its Creator was God, and He Himself pronounced it thus. All of life was sacred, from the first couple's evening prayers to their daily toil, and there was no distinction whatsoever between the secular and the sacred. Work was a divine vocation that was intended to build the kingdom of God by advancing culture and a godly civilization. "The Lord God took the man and put him in the Garden of Eden to work it and take care of it" (Genesis 2:15). This, of course, did not require evangelization since there was nothing from which one needed to be redeemed, so work was justified as worship simply in its own right. To Adam was given the dignity of naming the animals. This demonstrated his lordship over all that God had created and underscored his role as vice-regent under God. Also ordained by God for this project was the institution of the family. Just as His benediction had been earlier pronounced on the birds of the air, so the Creator turned to the creature He had made in His own image: "God blessed them and said to them, 'Be fruitful and increase in number; fill the earth and subdue it. Rule over the fish of the sea and the birds of the air and over every living creature that moves on the ground'" (Genesis 1:28). Rather than a burden to the earth, children were to be seen as a divine blessing and a means of upholding God's universal lordship over the created world. This dominion required stewardship and responsibility; surely the exploitation that has too often been associated with human dominion was far from the original task. Families were to be the center of this universal kingdom of God.

183

There was no need for government, as there was a perfect harmony between God's will and the rule of His creatures.

All of this changed, however, after the Fall. With rebellion, the single fabric of human life was torn. Where once work was linked solely to pleasure and worshipful joy in fulfilling God's purpose, now it was to involve "painful toil," and the blessing upon the family was overshadowed by the curse of painful childbirth. Enmity was placed between the husband and wife, and the war between Satan and the Son of Eve was announced (Genesis 3:14–20). No longer was the institution of marriage and the family to be considered necessarily holy or sacred, as the "house of the wicked" and the "house of the righteous" were now distinguished. Nor was work to be regarded as the building of God's kingdom. A godly civilization was now out of the question, as God removed His Paradise from earth back to heaven, driving man from the glorious temple of Eden: "After he drove the man out, he placed on the east side of the Garden of Eden cherubim and a flaming sword flashing back and forth to guard the way to the tree of life" (Genesis 3:24). In other words, "No Utopia on Earth" was scrawled above human history, crushing all human hopes of building the perfect society.

God did not leave Adam and Eve
without hope. Even in the face of
His judgment, He announced the Gospel.

This did not, of course, mean that human beings stopped believing in that vision, as we see later in the story.

In spite of all these curses upon normal human existence, including the division of the secular and sacred, God did not leave Adam and Eve without hope. Even in the face of His judgment, He announced the Gospel: After He declared the ultimate triumph of the Son of Man over Satan (Genesis 3:15), we read, "The Lord God made garments of skin for Adam and his wife and clothed them" (v. 21). Even though He would have been perfectly within His rights as a holy Judge to have carried out His sentence

184

of eternal death, God chose to have mercy on Adam and Eve and promised to them a coming Redeemer.

The good news, however, did not change the bad news for the world. In other words, by trusting in the coming Redeemer, the Son of Eve, the royal couple could be reconciled to God as heavenly Father and enjoy the eternal blessedness that they had been promised upon the condition of obedience, except now it was conditioned not on their obedience, but on the obedience and victory of that coming seed. Nevertheless, this did not restore Paradise, nor did it remove the curse God had announced upon the institutions and individuals of the fallen world. While they were embraced in God's eternal protection, they were banished from the Garden and were forced to live in this world no longer as princes who ruled the world as the realm of God's kingdom, but as strangers and aliens.

The story continues with the next generation: "Adam lay with his wife Eve, and she conceived and gave birth to Cain. She said, 'With the help of the Lord I have brought forth a man.' Later she gave birth to his brother Abel" (Genesis 4:1–2). Hebrew scholars have pointed out that Eve's response could also be translated, "With the help of the Lord I have brought forth *the* man." Either way, it is very likely that Eve thought that she had just given birth to the promised Messiah, since God's announcement had been concerning "your offspring," with no specific generation indicated. Given this interpretation, Eve must have been surprised to learn that this one upon whom she had set her hopes, instead of being her savior, had murdered his brother. The motive in this murder is itself instructive: "The Lord looked with favor on Abel and his offering, but on Cain and his offering he did not look with favor" (Genesis 4:4–5). It was the first religious squabble, and it concerned the matter of divine worship. Are we to devise any form of worship we prefer or the one which God has commanded? Animal sacrifices, such as the ones God had made to clothe Adam and Eve, were chosen by God to prefigure the Lamb of God who takes away the sin of the world. Furthermore, Abel selected "the firstborn of his flock" (v. 4), which God intended to foreshadow Christ, "the firstborn among many brothers" (Romans 8:29; Colossians 1:15, 18; Hebrews 1:6; Revelation 1:5). But Cain instead chose a sacrifice of vegetables. He had chosen his own way of salvation apart from Christ, apart from the promise, and God rejected him.

Cain's response, far from repentance, was anger, and it led him to persecute Abel, the true worshiper. Instead of seeing her Messiah, Eve saw the beginning of the prophesied curse concerning the enmity between Satan and her seed. For the rest of history, down to Herod's slaughter of the children in Israel, Satan would attempt to destroy the messianic seed and, with that seed, the hopes of redemption for God's people.

But here is the interesting point: Instead of destroying Cain then and there, God preserved his life, but issued this curse: "You will be a restless wanderer on the earth" (Genesis 4:12). Fearing that he would himself be killed in retribution, Cain cried out in horror at the prospect of being forever driven from God's protective presence. But God promised that He would place His mark on Cain "so that no one who found him would kill him." Why all this concern for a man who was guilty of murdering his brother? We learn as the story unfolds: "Cain lay with his wife, and she became pregnant and gave birth to Enoch. Cain was then building a city, and he named it after his son Enoch" (v. 17). The verses that follow walk us through the genealogy of these urban architects, informing us that Jabal was the father of ranching, Jubal "the father of all who play the harp and flute," and Tubal-Cain "forged all kinds of tools out of bronze and iron" (vv. 20–22). In other words, God preserved Cain for the purpose of building a city.

But then the story immediately turns to another son and another genealogy: "Adam lay with his wife again, and she gave birth to a son and named him Seth, saying, 'God has granted me another child in place of Abel, since Cain killed him.' Seth also had a son, and he named him Enosh. At that time men began to call on the name of the Lord" (vv. 25–26). Notice the contrast here: Cain's line begins with his son Enoch, while Cain was building a city; Seth's line begins with his son Enosh, when men began to call on the name of the Lord. Cain sought to end his restless wandering by building a city, while Seth set his hopes on an eternal city.

All of this is important if we want to see how the earliest chapters of the biblical record distinguish creation from redemption. Before the Fall, there is no such thing as redemption because there is no sin. There is no distinction between secular and sacred. But after the Fall, the city of God is taken back up into heaven, the earthly Paradise is "boarded up," and re-entry is guarded by the cherubim. God is still upholding, preserving, and advancing civilization by restraining the evil of the human heart, but no earthly city is to be confused with a godly civilization or with the kingdom of God.

This pattern is followed throughout the Old Testament. Even when God brings heaven to earth again in order to prefigure the coming kingdom of the Messiah, eventually Israel's failure to mirror God's will for humanity leads to its banishment. Once again, we read, an angel was posted at the eastern gate of the temple, forbidding entry, just as the eastern gate of Eden had been blocked.

One does not have to "bless" work or secular institutions with the adjective "Christian," or "redemptive," or "kingdom" for it to be honorable to God. That was the Reformation's point: not that there is no distinction between secular and sacred, for there is going to be a division between the kingdom of Christ and the kingdoms of this world until Christ's return, but that the secular realm is honorable because it has the same Creator and Sustainer as does the church itself. But Cain is always Cain, and the city of man never becomes the city of God until the end of history.

To be *in the world,* therefore, means that Christians and non-Christians work side by side, both bearing the divine image and equally capable of civil virtue, creativity, pleasure, pain, success, failure, wisdom, and kindness. An artist has no promise that his craft will improve and receive success upon his conversion.

But this is tremendously liberating for many of us who were led to believe that everything we did in work, in pleasure, in our artistic and creative or academic interests had to have some connection to evangelism or the church in order to justify our time and expense in those endeavors.

To be in the world *but not of the world* requires that we know the Christian faith well enough to recognize when we are allowing worldly definitions, attitudes, outlooks, and patterns to shape our beliefs and expressions.

Unbelievers, apart from divine special revelation, know right from wrong and are capable of wisdom and goodness in daily living. Whose experience does not teach him or her that there are wonderful people who really do care for people and try to do the right thing, even if they are not Christians? But that is "righteousness before men," not "righteousness before God." It is a *sinful* goodness because it does not conform to God's Law, and it is performed by someone who is not clothed in the righteousness of Christ alone. Even the good works of believers are stained with sin, so that Isaiah could lament, "Our *righteous* acts are like filthy rags" (Isaiah 64:6, italics added), let alone our sins! The only reason God accepts our works as good is that they are covered by Christ's righteousness and sweetened by His sacrifice.

Unless we understand the difference between common grace and saving grace, unbelievers will be led to presumption and believers will be led to doubt.

As we sometimes do not sufficiently appreciate our abiding sinfulness as Christians, we do not take the image of God in non-Christians seriously enough, I fear. Unlike Paul, who recognized that there was enough light in nature to hold the heathen accountable before God's judgment, we assume that there is a "Christian" way of painting, working, writing, researching, and rearing children that renders believers somehow automatically superior in these fields. Christians and non-Christians engage in these worldly pursuits on the same basis: They are both image-bearers who have received a divine calling to a particular post in creation. This would have been true had there been no Fall, no

Cross, and no redemption. But even after the Fall, the realm of creation is still enough to justify our activity in that realm.

Common Grace and Saving Grace

Still another helpful distinction, "common grace" explains how God sends rain to the just and the unjust alike and expects us to follow His example, while "saving grace" refers to the particular blessing God has given His people through faith in Christ.

When we confuse these two categories, it is easy to see success in business as a sign of divine favor and floods in a particular region as the sign of divine reprobation. Jesus was telling His disciples in Matthew chapter five that there is no direct correlation between God's judgment at the end of history and His providence here and now. The ungodly mistake God's common grace for saving grace by presuming that because things are not so bad right now, they are not under God's displeasure, while believers wonder, "Why do the wicked prosper?" (Psalm 73). Unless we understand the difference between common grace and saving grace, unbelievers will be led to presumption and believers will be led to doubt.

Therefore, unbelievers are capable of great things because (a) they still bear God's image, as truly as any Christian, and (b) they are gifted and held in check by God's general, superintending providence and common grace.

This means that if there are two men on the assembly line, one a Christian and the other an atheist, both are bringing glory to God by fulfilling their earthly calling. Whether a janitor or judge, artist or homemaker, manager or musician, every human being is meant to fulfill the goal of his or her creation: to glorify God and enjoy Him forever. The Fall did not erase that indelible mark on the human soul, however much we may attempt to efface it and rub out its impression. While the atheist may not set out to glorify God, the Creator "works out everything in conformity with the purpose of his will" (Ephesians 1:11). Even when His creatures are resolutely and violently set against Him, even that will serve God's glory: "Surely your wrath against men brings you praise, and the survivors of your wrath are restrained" (Psalm 76:10).

As God preserved Cain and, in His common grace, providentially governed the building of secular civilization, so He continues to superintend the construction of our earthly cities. It is when men and women, longing for the return to Eden, attempt to force a marriage between the city of God and the cities of this world that we see foreshadowings of the Last Judgment. With the Flood lingering in the collective memory as the most cataclysmic point in history, the civilization that emerged from Noah's descendants "had one language and a common speech," and decided to build a vast city on the plains of Shinar. "Then they said, 'Come, let us build ourselves a city, with a tower that reaches to the heavens, so that we may make a name for ourselves and not be scattered over the face of the whole earth" (Genesis 11:4).

The purpose of this metroplex was to create a tower that would be so high that any future flood could not reach them. Instead of trusting in God's promise not to judge the world by flood, with the rainbow as the sacrament of the divine oath, these architects of civilization took their salvation into their own hands and built a city whose express purpose was to redeem its inhabitants. While it is true that, "What God hath joined together, let not man divide," the reverse is also true: What God hath divided, let no man join together. Not only were human beings not to re-enter Eden; they also were not to establish a heaven on earth ever again wherever they went. But the Tower of Babel was a religious building. As Cain refused to worship God through his appointed means of blood sacrifice, the builders of this very religiously secular city refused to receive salvation from God. Instead of trusting in His promise, they sought to save themselves by the technology of their own hands.

God's response was swift and conclusive. As they were building a tower toward the heavens, God descended from the heavens in judgment. They were building up and God was coming down. "So the Lord scattered them from there over all the earth, and they stopped building the city. That is why it was called Babel—because there the Lord confused the language of the whole world. From there the Lord scattered them over the face of the whole earth" (Genesis 11:8–9).

Similarly today, we have seen the collapse of perhaps the grandest attempt to save the world through civilization since that ancient episode. Cheerfully casting aside the "superstitions" of revealed religion, the Enlightenment substituted human reason, willpower, and know-how, promising a new Canaan for all who would join hearts and hands in the enterprise. Our age has also forgotten (or suppressed the fact) that "salvation comes from the Lord" (Jonah 2:9), and has again confused the building of earthly civilizations with the reconstruction of an earthly paradise. We see in the "Christian" empires of Rome, Germany, Britain, and America the dangers inherent in confusing the power, glory, and honor of the earthly city with that of the heavenly Jerusalem.

In the New Testament, Jesus announced, "My kingdom is not of this world. If it were, my servants would fight to prevent my arrest by the Jews. But now my kingdom is from another place" (John 18:36). No longer is God's kingdom identified with a plot of land, whether Eden or Israel. The church is composed of Jews and Gentiles who have, like Abel, worshiped the Lamb of God who takes away the sin of the world and, like Seth's descendants, have called upon the name of the Lord. These may not be the great architects of civilization, for they are content to wander as strangers in this world. Even Israel was not the ultimate "promised land" for Abraham and his descendants: "By faith [Abraham] made his home in the promised land like a stranger in a foreign country; he lived in tents, as did Isaac and Jacob, who were heirs with him of the same promise. For he was looking forward to the city with foundations, whose architect and builder is God" (Hebrews 11:9–10). Although those living in the earthly Promised Land never saw the final rest and the things promised for which we are still looking, they "welcomed them from a distance" (v. 13). They were not willing to place their ultimate hopes even in the Promised Land. "Instead, they were longing for a better country—a heavenly one. Therefore God is not ashamed to be called their God, for he has prepared a city for them" (v. 16).

The spiritual children of Cain have the light of nature to guide them in their building of civilization; the spiritual descendants of Seth have the light of Scripture and the mind of Christ. Unbelievers may build great cities and be guided in their efforts by God's gracious providence, but believers must be content to wander as strangers and pilgrims. They must be content with their nomadic existence in this world.

This, then, is the tension we find in Scripture. By creation, we are engaged in a common task, joined in common experiences, and linked by common bonds with unbelievers. This means that we are not to regard this world as alien because it is *the world* rather than *heaven,* but because it is presently in rebellion against God. We, still at war with rebellion in our own hearts, long for the day of final redemption when at long last "the kingdoms of this world are become the kingdoms of our Lord, and of his Christ; and he shall reign for ever and ever" (Revelation 11:15 KJV).

We already have some foreshadowings of this great event. Just as God descended in judgment upon the secular salvation of the Tower of Babel by confusing the languages and dividing the nations, so at Pentecost He descended in salvation upon the church by allowing each man and woman who had arrived in Jerusalem from the far-flung nations for the feast to hear the Gospel in his or her own native tongue. This was not meant to announce the beginning of a new theocracy, the direct reign of God through a particular earthly nation, but it was a signpost of the spiritual kingdom that has already arrived in Christ and awaits its consummation when the city of man once again becomes sacred, the city of God.

Until then, we must wait. But waiting does not mean that we are inactive or apathetic. Although Joseph and Daniel were part of that spiritual seed of wanderers rather than of civilization-builders, each was able to use his position to honor God in secular leadership. Joseph and Daniel are good examples of Christians in secular government, yet they did not seek to turn their respective offices into catalysts for making the kingdoms of this world biblical theocracies as Israel had been. They simply pursued their calling in the world with excellence and diligence, winning the respect of their foreign rulers and improving the lives of those over whom they exercised authority. This is exactly what Paul tells the Thessalonians in their "Babylonian captivity," exiled from the heavenly city for a time (1 Thessalonians 4:11).

Regardless of one's calling, then, each of us is expected to pursue excellence in the realm of creation, alongside unbelievers, and this secular calling is just as noble as the sacred calling to the ministry of Word and sacrament. Believers are holy because they belong to Christ, but the realm to which they are called is common. They are expected to themselves be distinct in their beliefs, attitudes, and lifestyles, but they are not to expect to convert their secular environment into a sacred space. When making decisions in court, Joseph and Daniel were bound to base their judgments on Egyptian and Babylonian law, not on Hebrew law, and while they were neither to endorse nor participate in anything that violated God's Word, they were free to accept the idea that they were called to serve pagan nations by a God who had uniquely gifted them for that purpose.

These facts are essential if we are to avoid the danger of confusing the secular and the sacred. There is a tendency in many circles today to speak in the following terms: "All of life is sacred," "all activity is 'kingdom activity,'" and so forth. This was true in Eden and it was true in the Jewish theocracy, but *now*, Jesus said, "my kingdom is from another place. It is no longer of this world." All of life is not sacred, but that which is simply common (i.e., "secular") is nevertheless valuable and honorable because it is part of God's creation. He is as much the Lord of the secular as He is of the sacred. Political activity is not "kingdom work," but the advance of the earthly cities was the original task given to Adam and his posterity in the cultural mandate. It is *secular* work that is, nevertheless, ordained and commanded by God. Therefore, Christians and non-Christians alike, bearing the divine image, pursue this cultural mandate—the former acknowledging it as *God's* mandate, the latter finding some other justification, but either way, that cultural mandate remains in effect. God's people have a particular duty to participate in the building of culture, since it was initially committed to humanity by their Creator *and* Redeemer. Nevertheless, the kingdom is not America or various cultural, academic, or political pursuits. These are secular callings that have God's blessing by virtue of creation, not "kingdom activities" that have God's blessing by virtue of redemption.

What does all of this mean, then, for our life in this world? It means that the Christian artist no longer has to justify his or her calling by the extent to which it makes a spiritual, religious, moral, evangelistic, or church-related point. It does not have to redeem; it simply has to entertain and express artistic excellence. The Christian musician does not have to write "Christian music" or sing "Gospel melodies," but he or she is free to create or perform secular music purely for human enjoyment and pleasure. Of course, such a person is still a Christian in all of this, and it is neither desirable nor possible to separate one's deepest spiritual convictions from one's work; nevertheless, it does not have to explicitly reveal those convictions in order to be an acceptable form of expression by a Christian. The Bible does reveal guidelines for Christian conduct in business and in human relationships. For instance, it may not be a guide to dating, but it does give us commands for treating others with dignity and respect and sexual purity; it may not be a manual for business success, but it does tell Christians how they must conduct themselves in such relationships, avoiding debt, dealing honestly, and building a future for their children.

However, a Christian plumber does not have to install "Christian" pipes, nor does a Christian judge have to open a session of court with a prayer and "Christianize" the courtroom with Bible readings. These specifically Christian forms of worship, education, and piety are to be inculcated in the Christian home and church. While this does not free us from being Christians in the secular arena and exonerate us from exercising our responsibilities as believers, it does mean that we can stop feeling guilty for simply doing our jobs to the best of our ability without being able to measure that success in terms of conversions to Christ or moral victories in the workplace.

It also means that we should not have to justify everything that we believe or do on the basis of Scripture. At first, that may sound surprising, so let me explain. The Bible does not tell us how to change the oil in our automobile, nor does it provide a guide to navigating the oceans or skies; it does not explain the circulation of blood or the circulation of Los Angeles freeways. (In fact, *nothing* really explains the circulation of Los Angeles freeways.) There are many aspects of child-rearing that are not covered in Scripture and a great deal about the practical matters of "things earthly" that the Bible has left to human discovery.

The Bible is concerned with that which cannot be discovered in nature: the Gospel of Jesus Christ, as it unfolds from Genesis to Revelation. It does not tell us what we can discover for ourselves but in greater detail or with greater wisdom; it tells us something we could never have learned through our own investigation, wisdom, or insight.

Just today in the religion section of one of our southern California newspapers, I read an article with the following heading: "Baby Feeding Based on Bible Stirs Debate." The article discusses a "Bible-based" guide to strictly scheduled feeding times for babies. Yet the book does not cite specific passages. In fact, the authors admit that there are none. But they list basic scriptural principles that cannot be ignored: "Order, sound judgment, love, patience, care, strong marriages and sober-minded assessment." Is there any reason that one should regard these principles as specifically biblical? Could not any person, Christian or non-Christian, come up with the same list? And does not this drive to see the Bible chiefly as the answer book, rule book, and instruction manual for life end up trivializing the real message of the Scriptures?

Furthermore, what happens when child psychologists or pediatricians determine that the "principles" which are deduced from these (supposedly) uniquely inspired general principles are actually harmful to babies? Is it another case of the Bible versus science? Of course not. Although that may indeed, unfortunately, be the way it is seen by those who do not know the Bible well enough to realize that it does not propose child-feeding principles, it is rather the case of the Christian author versus science, while the Bible is a casualty of "friendly fire."

This is an extreme example of what is a rather common tendency in contemporary evangelicalism to demand that the Bible be "relevant" by making it say things in which it does not have the slightest interest. We trivialize the Scriptures when we ignore its real message, which is doctrinal, and instead squeeze applications to daily life from verses that were never intended to yield quite so much "relevant" data.

If we know God's Word well enough, we will be able to detect the problems in a book by a secular child psychologist, but that does not mean that the Bible is intended to replace that practical book which, in many ways, helps parents to understand their children. The Scriptures are sufficient for everything related to saving truth and for the revelation of God's moral will, but they were never intended to be sufficient for everything else. We do not need a Christian view of auto mechanics or biblical principles for open-heart surgery, so why do we need Christian music, Christian books, Christian art, or Christian businesses? Sacred music (for instance, hymns) and art that is specifically designed for use in worship (for instance, architecture) serve a unique function, and these are unique styles—*church* music and *church* architecture. But do we really need Christian pop music for our entertainment or Christian cookbooks? Is there really a Christian method of making stir-fry? This brings us to another important and closely related point.

Natural Revelation and Special Revelation

Not only are unbelievers aware of God's attributes, but they also know God's Law: "Although they know God's righteous decree that those who do such things deserve death, they not only continue to do these very things but also approve of those who practice them" (Romans 1:32). Therefore, "When Gentiles, who do not have the law, do by nature things required by the law, they are a law for themselves, even though they do not have the law, since they show that the requirements of the law are written on their hearts, their consciences also bearing witness, and their thoughts now accusing, now even defending them" (Romans 2:14–15).

As there is a sufficient basis for a "natural theology"—that is, a discussion of divine attributes from the created world—there is a sufficient basis for "natural law"—a discussion of right and wrong, truth and error, justice and corruption, beauty and horror, crime and punishment—even with nothing more than the human conscience. The Gentiles, Paul argues, are even capable of conforming externally to this law written on their consciences. This is what the Reformers called "civil righteousness, virtue, justice." It was how they understood the wisdom of Seneca's jurisprudence, the beauty of Homer's epic poetry, and the marvel of astronomical advances. Their virtue, however, is purely "civil"—that is, it serves the city of man, as Cain's descendants produced great advances in civilization even though they were banished from the city of God. The only virtue that God accepts as righteous is perfect conformity of will, heart, mind, affections, and actions to His own holiness. Therefore, this civil righteousness is but "filthy rags" before the divine judgment (Isaiah 64:6). Nevertheless, it is that external, purely civil virtue that explains how unbelievers can build reasonably just civilizations, with grand artistic, literary, scientific, and legal traditions. Paul even drew upon his knowledge of secular Greek poetry and philosophy in order to build bridges to unbelievers in Athens (Acts 17:16 ff).

Here is where the Reformation freed men and women who had been led to believe that, unless they were engaged in "full-time Christian ministry" or could somehow use their art in the service of the church, they were second-class Christians. It was not by insisting that their work be specifically "Christian" in any explicit sense, but by reminding them of God's blessing over creation in its own right, that many believers were liberated from churchly constraints to glorify God and enjoy Him in their callings.

Governments were also free from having to adopt Old Testament civil law as their own. After all, the giving of the written law was a divine ceremony between God and His people after their redemption from the land of slavery. The nations have God's law written in their conscience, but the people of God have God's law written in Scripture, Calvin argues: "For the Lord through the hand of Moses did not give that law to be proclaimed among all nations and to be in force everywhere; but when he had taken the Jewish nation into safekeeping, defense, and protection, he also willed to be a lawgiver especially unto it."[2]

As these ideas of "natural law" had been somewhat controversial when Thomas Aquinas articulated them in the thirteenth century, so they were not terribly welcome in Calvin's day. Nevertheless, the Reformer was simply unpacking Paul's description of human nature: If the Law of God is written on the conscience of the pagan who has never been acquainted with the Scriptures, then unbelievers can establish reasonably just societies.

We resist being told what to believe and
how to live—even if God is doing the talking.

Throughout the Middle Ages, for instance, the practice of charging interest on loans was considered a violation of the Old Testament law against usury (Leviticus 25:36), but Calvin, distinguishing between the *civil, ceremonial,* and *moral* laws of Israel, argued that the first two categories were limited to Israel as a unique theocratic institution foreshadowing the coming kingdom. Just as the ceremonial laws are fulfilled and, therefore, are not to be enforced in the church or in society, the civil laws have a unique and temporary sign-bearing reference to the nation of Israel under the Old Covenant. Therefore, the Reformer convinced the civil authorities that they were no longer bound by this command against charging interest, so long as equity (justice) prevailed in administering it. To that end, the poor were not charged interest, but those with modest or wealthy means were charged low interest. This encouraged loans, which, in turn, encouraged economic growth for all. When the church enforced Old Testament civil legislation on what it regarded as the *Holy* Roman Empire, Calvin accused the church of "mingling heaven and earth."

But this recovery of such important distinctions also led Luther, Calvin, and other Reformers to encourage the liberation of the arts, sciences, and other disciplines from the oversight of the church. Just as the confusion had led many to deny the validity of secular legislation, many denied the validity of secular wisdom, philosophy, science, and art.

But as God gave wisdom to Daniel to understand secular literature and philosophy, so He graciously gives His common grace to all men and women bearing His image. It is not saving knowledge or saving wisdom, but it is a gift of the Holy Spirit nonetheless. Apart from this work of the Spirit in creation and providence, the world would be ugly, tyrannical, unjust, and unhappy—with absolutely no insight, education, laughter, pleasure, delight, or singing.

By seeking the interests of our clients or constituents and not using our job or office as a bully-pulpit for our faith, we will win the respect of outsiders—and this, according to the apostle Paul, is a noble goal. By pursuing excellence in art and music, if that is our calling, and not using our crafts merely as a means of preaching, teaching, evangelizing, or rebuking, we bring a smile to the face of the God who created beauty and pleasure as acceptable in its own right.

REBUILDING THE FOUNDATIONS

Many people today, whether believers or unbelievers, view "systems" of belief with great suspicion. The sociologist Wade Clark Roof has recently reminded us that Americans like "spirituality" but not "religion," and by that Americans mean that they like to shape gods of their own experience; they view religion as requiring a particular creed and set of dogmas, along with a moral code of divine expectations. Democratic to the very core, we resist being told what to believe and how to live—even if God is doing the talking.

That is an understandable sentiment in some ways. Many unchurched folks today grew up in restrictive, legalistic, and dogmatic environments where they were not encouraged to ask questions, doubt, raise objections, or make decisions about their personal behavior. But this feeling is deeper than mere reaction; it is part of human nature, ever since the Fall, to sing with Frank Sinatra, "I did it my way."

What I hope to have demonstrated, in some modest way, is the importance of rebuilding the foundations of our faith. Apart from a transcendent theological framework, anything that we build will be haphazard and, like the house in our Lord's parable, will be built on the sands of personal whim and social fad only to be washed out to sea. At present, many Christians—even Christian leaders—scoff at the critics who point to the sandy foundation. Encouraged by the high walls, they insist that no enemy can penetrate the godly citadel; proud of the grandeur of the castle's scale, they reply, "How can you argue with success?" And yet, the rains will come, and all of the crusades and movements of the last forty years will be easily forgotten. What will stand are not our own sand castles, however impressive by worldly standards, but the house that is built on the Rock. It is time for Christians who take the Bible seriously to take what the Bible regards as serious with equal seriousness, and the Bible takes theology with utmost seriousness.

Church officers are given, not to build larger churches with an impressive array of programs and entertaining "celebrations," but "to prepare God's people for works of service, so that the body of Christ may be built up until we all reach unity in the faith and in the knowledge of the Son of God and become mature, attaining to the whole measure of the fullness of Christ. Then we will no longer be infants, tossed back and forth by the waves, and blown here and there by every wind of teaching and by the cunning and craftiness of men in their deceitful scheming" (Ephesians 4:12–14). Note that we are prepared for works of service and the body is built up, not by superficial calls to action or pleas for unity, but by the very thing that so many pastors and laypeople today think is the very obstacle to those goals: doctrine. Paul calls us to "unity in *the faith*," not just an experience of faith, but to *the* faith "and in the *knowledge* of the Son of God." This is precisely what theology is, the building up of the body of Christ in the faith and in the knowledge of the Son of God. Without it, the church cannot survive, much less transform the culture. At present, we are tossed back and forth with every new teaching, from the signs and wonders movement and pop-psychology fads to political crusades; from strange views and predictions of the Second Coming to remarkably unorthodox views of salvation.

Not only does Scripture place a high priority on getting our beliefs straight and developing a systematic theology; history proves again and again that the church's practice in any age is never better than its theory. (Usually its practice falls somewhere short of its theory.) Our theology (i.e., understanding of Scripture's basic teachings) forms the spectacles through which we view the world; without them our outlook is blurry, distorted, fragmented. We know what it is like to have our physical vision impaired: It not only makes life frustrating, but it also makes us ill-prepared to explain what we see. We become dependent on the vision of other people. If we are to become faithful both as churchmen and women and also as citizens and workers in the world, we will have to recover our biblical spectacles.

Throughout this brief survey we have seen how the theology of the Reformation—by no means original with the Reformers of the sixteenth century—actually gave rise to so many of the blessings of the modern world that have, by modernity's repudiation of that basis, become curses and idols of contemporary society. Politics, the arts, education, science, work, and leisure have not only lost their meaning, but they have also become actively engaged in breaking down the modern man or woman's delight in being human. As André Malraux, the French existentialist, explained to the General Assembly of the United Nations nearly three decades ago, "The theologians have announced that God is dead, and now the rest of us must announce the death of man."

If we wish to recover a sense of the sacred, it will not be by turning to these idols for their favors, but by turning our backs on them entirely. I am not saying we must stay out of these arenas—far from it—but I am saying that we must stop looking for handouts and protection from them. Political entitlement and moral legislation, artistic propaganda, educational indoctrination, belligerence in the scientific community, and antagonism at work will not change anything; these tactics only serve to give credence to the caricatures.

When keys are lost, the most common advice is to retrace one's steps: "Where did you have them last?" The same is true when the church has lost its bearings, as it has in our day. The culture that was shaped in large measure by a Reformation worldview has been unraveling ever since the triumph of the Enlightenment and the beliefs and structures of modern life that it produced. Although the Reformation was hardly perfect, God graciously returned the church to its proper course. The results, though not pursued as the *purpose* for the Reformation, were incalculable in their good to the culture. And the effects continue to be felt in every discipline and enterprise to the present day.

University of Paris historian Pierre Chaunu remarks, "Yes, we are fashioned by the world of the Reformation."[3] Harvard historian Steven Ozment credits the Reformation with the recovery of literacy and the centrality of the family in social organizations. In fact, he observes that the Reformation "was a struggle with many of the same problems that grip us today. . . . Whether one views the Reformation in terms of its literature, its laws, or the lives of the laity who embraced it, it portrays itself as the hand that interrupts unrealistic dreams and exposes false prophets. Protestant faith promised to save people above all from disabling credulity."[4]

Stanford's Lewis Spitz has remarked of the Reformation that "few periods in the long history of Europe have had such a momentous impact upon the western world,"[5] and Yale's Roland Bainton noted, "Luther, as no one before him in more than a thousand years, sensed the import of the miracle of divine forgiveness. . . . The Reformation was a religious revival. Its attempt was to give man a new assurance in the presence of God and a new motivation in the moral life."[6] Oxford historian Owen Chadwick added, "The Reformation age, amid grievous destruction, swept away the clutter, pursued simplicity of vision, and directed the gaze of the worshipper towards that which truly mattered. After Luther it was not possible for either Protestant or Catholic to imitate some of the old ways of neglecting God's grace and sovereignty."[7]

It was out of this recovery of "first things" that Christianity not only gained a new hold over millions in a decaying and secularizing "Christendom," but it was allowed to create massive improvements in the culture as well. Reformed Christians restored Oxford and Cambridge and founded Harvard, Yale, Princeton, Dartmouth, Brown, Rutgers, and a host of other universities as far away as Asia and Africa. These were the same people, however, who launched the modern missionary movement as well as modern science. As the missionary heart of these Reformation heirs beat fervently for the lost around the globe, cultures were also transformed in the bargain. For them, there was a perfect harmony between the world and the Bible, reason and faith, doctrine and life. Look at every arena of confusion and disrepair in our day: education, health care, science, the arts and entertainment, philosophy and theology, the family. The Reformation revolutionized these spheres once, and, if its rich resources are tapped again and brought to bear on the unique circumstances of contemporary life and struggles, it could have a similar effect in our own time.

But today, not only are we finding that Christian (or indeed any religious) claims for truth fall on deaf ears in the culture, we find decay in the church itself and a greater interest in success than in faithfulness.

If we are to see the culture change, we must look first to the body of Christ, beginning with our own families. I realize that this sounds escapist, but it is nothing of the kind. Nor is it to suggest that we should leave our secular occupations and become church workers; I have argued against that expectation throughout this work. But it is to say that before we can change the culture, we must recover the purity of doctrine and life that has always had a transformative influence in the world. We must stop accommodating to the very culture that we are opposing and attempting to transform. To do that we must not only know our own theology, but we must also know the idols and understand the ways in which we ourselves are shaped more by the spirit of the age than by the Spirit of Christ. As families and churches learn the "whole counsel of God" all over again and recover the Law and the Gospel in the diet of preaching, teaching, and worship, there will be a fresh integrity to the church's witness before a cynical world that has forgotten the last time it took the church seriously.

We should not expect to merely resurrect the Protestant Reformers or naively imitate that movement. There are unique challenges in our day, and our postmodern age presents a different context from that of premodern Europe. But the basic ideas are the same and are there for the taking. The Reformation did not set out to change the culture, yet it is credited in varying degrees with the rise of democracy and human rights, modern science, the revival of arts and letters, the foundation of some of the world's leading universities, laying the seeds for the modern missionary movement, and liberating views of work, leisure, and the family. Conversely, many Christian movements today set out to change the culture, but they end up being changed by the culture —taken captive themselves, because the roots were too shallow.

Wherever there are Christians in the world who still care about truth and its impact in a culture of decay, there will always be an interest in theology. No wonder Columbia University historian Eugene F. Rice, Jr., could remark that the Reformation's theology "strikingly measures the gulf between the secular imagination of the twentieth century and sixteenth-century Protestantism's intoxication with the majesty of God. We can only exercise historical sympathy to try to understand how it was that many of the most sensitive intelligences of a whole epoch found a supreme, a total, liberty in the abandonment of human weakness to the omnipotence of God."[8]

May God grant the same consciousness to His people in our time, for God's sake and for the sake of the world.

NOTES

1. Philipp Jakob Spener, "Christian Joy," in *Pietists: Selected Writings* (London: Paulist/SPCK, 1983), 96.

2. John Calvin, *Institutes,* 4.20.8–14.

3. Pierre Chaunu, *The Reformation* (New York: St. Martin's, 1986), 14.

4. Steven Ozment, *When Fathers Ruled: Family Life in Reformation Europe* (Cambridge: Harvard Univ., 1983) and *Protestants: The Birth of a Revolution* (New York: Doubleday, 1992).

5. Lewis Spitz, *The Protestant Reformation: The Rise of Modern Europe* (New York: Harper, 1985), 1.

6. Cited in Hans Hillerbrand, *Men and Ideas in the Sixteenth Century* (Chicago: Rand McNally, 1969), 2.

7. Ibid.

8. Eugene F. Rice, Jr., *The Foundations of Modern Europe* (New York: Norton, 1970), 136.

INDEX